EUROPE'S REFUGEE CRISIS: HOW SHOULD THE U.S., EU, AND OSCE RESPOND?

I0423673

HEARING

BEFORE THE

COMMISSION ON SECURITY AND COOPERATION IN EUROPE

ONE HUNDRED FOURTEENTH CONGRESS

FIRST SESSION

OCTOBER 20, 2015

Printed for the use of the
Commission on Security and Cooperation in Europe

[CSCE 114–1–5]

U.S. GOVERNMENT PUBLISHING OFFICE

97–466 PDF   WASHINGTON : 2015

For sale by the Superintendent of Documents, U.S. Government Publishing Office
Internet: bookstore.gpo.gov   Phone: toll free (866) 512–1800; DC area (202) 512–1800
Fax: (202) 512–2104   Mail: Stop IDCC, Washington, DC 20402–0001

COMMISSION ON SECURITY AND COOPERATION IN EUROPE

LEGISLATIVE BRANCH COMMISSIONERS

HOUSE

CHRISTOPHER H. SMITH, New Jersey,
  Chairman
ALCEE L. HASTINGS, Florida
ROBERT B. ADERHOLT, Alabama
MICHAEL C. BURGESS, Texas
STEVE COHEN, Tennessee
ALAN GRAYSON, Florida
RANDY HULTGREN, Illinois
JOSEPH R. PITTS, Pennsylvania
LOUISE McINTOSH SLAUGHTER,
  New York

SENATE

ROGER F. WICKER, Mississippi,
  Co-Chairman
BENJAMIN L. CARDIN, Maryland
JOHN BOOZMAN, Arkansas
RICHARD BURR, North Carolina
JEANNE SHAHEEN, New Hampshire
TOM UDALL, New Mexico
SHELDON WHITEHOUSE, Rhode Island

EXECUTIVE BRANCH COMMISSIONERS

Vacant, Department of State
Vacant, Department of Commerce
Vacant, Department of Defense

[II]

EUROPE'S REFUGEE CRISIS: HOW SHOULD THE U.S., EU, AND OSCE RESPOND?

COMMISSIONERS

WITNESSES

APPENDICES

EUROPE'S REFUGEE CRISIS: HOW SHOULD THE U.S., EU, AND OSCE RESPOND?

October 20, 2015

COMMISSION ON SECURITY AND COOPERATION IN EUROPE

WASHINGTON, DC

The hearing was held at 1:59 p.m. in room 2200, Rayburn House Office Building, Washington, DC, Hon. Christopher H. Smith, Chairman, Commission on Security and Cooperation in Europe, presiding.

Commissioners present: Hon. Christopher H. Smith, Chairman, Commission on Security and Cooperation in Europe; Hon. Joe Pitts, Commissioner, Commission on Security and Cooperation in Europe; Hon. Michael Burgess, Commissioner, Commission on Security and Cooperation in Europe; Hon. Jeanne Shaheen, Commissioner, Commission on Security and Cooperation in Europe; Hon. John Boozman, Commissioner, Commission on Security and Cooperation in Europe; Hon. Randy Hultgren, Commissioner, Commission on Security and Cooperation in Europe; and Hon. Steve Cohen, Commissioner, Commission on Security and Cooperation in Europe.

Witnesses present: Anne C. Richard, Assistant Secretary, Bureau of Population, Refugees, and Migration, U.S. Department of State; Shelley Pitterman, Regional Representative to the United States and Caribbean, Office of the United Mations High Commissioner for Refugees (UNHCR); Djerdj Matković, Ambassador of the Republic of Serbia to the United States; Sean Callahan, Chief Operating Officer, Catholic Relief Services; and David O'Sullivan, Ambassador of the European Union to the United States.

HON. CHRISTOPHER H. SMITH, CHAIRMAN, COMMISSION ON SECURITY AND COOPERATION IN EUROPE

Mr. SMITH. [Sounds gavel.] The Commission will come to order, and I want to wish you all a very pleasant afternoon. And welcome to this hearing as we inquire into the European refugee crisis and how the U.S., the EU and the OSCE should respond.

The Syrian displacement crisis that has consumed seven countries in the Middle East has become the biggest refugee crisis in Europe since World War II. At least 250,000 people have been killed in Syria's civil war, many of them civilians. The security forces of Syrian dictator Bashir al-Assad have been responsible for many of these killings, targeting neighborhoods with barrel bombs and shooting civilians point blank. ISIS has committed genocide, mass atrocities, and war crimes against Christians and other mi-

(1)

norities, and likewise targeted, brutalized, and killed Shia and Sunni Muslims who reject its ideology and its brutality.

Fleeing for safety, more than 4 million Syrians are refugees, the largest refugee population in the world, and another 7.6 million Syrians are displaced inside their home country. Syria's neighbors—Jordan, Lebanon, Turkey, Iraq, and Egypt—are hosting most of these refugees. Before the Syria crisis, these countries struggled with high rates of unemployment, strained public services, and a range of other domestic challenges. Since the conflict began, Syrian refugees have become a quarter of Lebanon's population. And Iraq, which has been beset by ISIS and sectarian conflict, is hosting almost 250,000 refugees from Syria.

Until this past summer, few Syrian refugees went beyond countries that border their homeland. Syrian refugees and migrants from a range of countries have since come to Europe in such large numbers, and so quickly, that many European countries—especially frontline entry points like Greece, transit countries like Serbia, and destination countries like Germany—have been challenged and even overwhelmed.

The U.N. High Commission for Refugees—the UNHCR—reports that more than 635,000 refugees and migrants have arrived in Europe by sea in 2015 alone. Fifty-three percent of these people are from Syria, 16 percent from Afghanistan, 6 percent from Eritrea, and 5 percent from Iraq. Notably, only 14 percent of them are women. Twenty percent are children, and the remaining 65 percent are men.

The European crisis requires a response that is European, national, and international. And the United States, we believe, is essential to it. There must be effective coordination and communication directly between countries, as well as through and with entities like the OSCE and the European Union. Individual countries also must have the flexibility to respond best to the particular circumstances in their own countries.

The response must address push factors like economic challenges and aid shortfalls in countries like Syria's neighbors that have been hosting refugees. As a matter of fact, Shelly Pitterman from the UNHCR said that one of the triggers, if not *the* trigger—as he put it, the last straw for some—was the humanitarian shortfall, especially the World Food Programme's cut of 30 percent in recent months. There also, again, we must address the pull factors, like decisions individual European countries have made that have attracted refugees.

There is real human need and desperation. We all know it, and that's why we're meeting. Refugees are entrusting themselves to smugglers, and where there is human smuggling there is also a higher risk of human trafficking. I am especially concerned about the risk of abuse, exploitation, and enslavement of women and children. Already we are hearing reports that some European countries are failing to protect women and girls from sexual assault and forced prostitution. The lack of separate bathroom facilities, for example, for males and females, rooms that can be locked, and other basic measures enable such attacks. There is no excuse for such failures, and everything must be done to ensure that women and children are safe.

There is also the real threat that terrorist groups like ISIS will infiltrate these massive movements of people to kill civilians in Europe and beyond. I am deeply concerned that the screening at many European borders still—and again, this is a crisis that was thrust upon them—but remain inadequate, putting lives at risk. All of us must be responsive to the humanitarian needs without compromising one iota on security. European response plans should include specifics about strengthening security screening throughout the European region.

During the conflict in Kosovo, I travelled to Stenkovec Refugee Camp in Macedonia—parenthetically, CRS was leading the effort there—and then was at the McGuire Air Force Base in New Jersey later on to welcome some of the 4,400 people brought from there to the United States. One refugee, however—Agron Abdullahu—was apprehended and sent to jail in 2008 for supplying guns and ammunition to the Fort Dix Five, a group of terrorists who were also sent to prison for plotting to kill American soldiers at the Fort Dix military installation, also in New Jersey.

Given Secretary Kerry's announcement in September that the United States intended to resettle at least 85,000 refugees in fiscal year 2016—including at least 10,000 Syrians—and at least 100,000 refugees in fiscal year 2017, the United States and Europe must be on high alert to weed out terrorists from real refugees. Because religious and ethnic minorities often have additional risks and vulnerabilities even as refugees, they should be prioritized for resettlement.

This hearing will examine the *who* is arriving, the *why* they are coming to Europe, and the *what* has been done and should be done in response. European governments, entities like the OSCE and EU, religiously based entities and civil society all have critical roles to play. The United States has been a leading donor to the humanitarian crisis inside Syria and refugee crises in the region. We also have the largest refugee admissions program in the world.

However, according to testimony of Shelly Pitterman again, regional rep of U.N. High Commission for Refugees—we'll hear from him shortly—the current interagency Syrian Regional Refugee and Resilience Plan for 2015, or the 3RP, is only 41 percent funded, which has meant cuts in food aid for thousands of refugees. Globally, he warns, the humanitarian system is financially broke. We are no longer able to meet even the absolute minimum requirements of core protection and life-saving assistance to preserve the human dignity of the people we care for.

The current level of funding, he goes on to say, for the 33 U.N. appeals to provide humanitarian assistance to some 82 million people around the world is only 42 percent—in other words, almost a 60 percent shortfall. UNHCR expects to receive just 47 percent of the funding they need in the next year.

Again, this hearing will look at how the United States can best work with our allies in Europe to meet humanitarian needs and prevent security threats. In the 20th and 21st centuries, the United States and Europe have come together to address the great challenges of our time, and this is an opportunity to do so again.

Before we begin, and before I yield to Dr. Burgess, I'd like to recognize Ambassador Dr. Reka Szemerkenyi, who is present here in the room today—and thank you, Madam Ambassador, for joining us for this hearing.

I'd like to now yield to Dr. Burgess. Then I will—Commissioner Pitts?

HON. JOSEPH PITTS, COMMISSIONER, COMMISSION ON SECURITY AND COOPERATION IN EUROPE

Mr. PITTS. Thank you, Mr. Chairman.

I want to thank fellow commissioners and distinguished panelists and guests. I want to thank all of you for your participation here today on this hearing on Europe's refugee crisis.

The term "crisis" does little justice to the dire situation that refugees are facing. The war in Syria, where more than half of the population has either been killed or displaced, has been raging for over four years now. The war's ensuing expansion and related brutality in neighboring countries have left millions of victims with no choice but to leave the lands that some groups have called home for thousands of years.

Many have observed this to constitute the greatest migration and refugee crisis since World War II, and this is especially troubling when you factor in the relatively small scale of the populations and regions in conflict. However, the roots of this crisis go far beyond the war in Syria, as witnessed by the participants in the migration flows. People from across the Middle East, Africa, Afghanistan, South Asia, and even the Balkans are contributing to this mass exodus from areas of strife. Among them are economic migrants, refugees, asylum seekers, and stateless people.

The numbers of migrants are increasing. It's estimated that over 500,000 have crossed into EU borders this year alone. Fatalities, too, are increasing at alarming rates. More than 3,500 perished in the Mediterranean last year, and this year possibly more than that will perish.

The OSCE can play a unique role in addressing this crisis, and help alleviate human suffering and mitigate related human rights abuses. The organization is uniquely equipped with tools, mandates, and a neutral framework that can help member states addressing an array of issues.

With Russia's direct entrance into the war in Syria, the OSCE's neutral framework could be of great use in reporting in Syria and the surrounding region. Furthermore, its relationship with the UNHCR can be of great significance to U.S. interests, as we rely on that institution for information on our own domestic resettlement processes.

I look forward to hearing about greater areas of cooperation in tackling this crisis. I want to thank all of the panelists here for their participation.

We must not forget that people are dying. As the U.S., the EU, and OSCE debate this issue, we must not let fear be the greatest motivator of our responses. The United States and the West must offer a stark contrast to ISIS and the Assad regime and other governments or terrorists that wreak havoc on religious and ethnic minorities, or other countless victims of human rights abuses that drive this crisis. We must carry a firm resolve that justice and charity is done under our watch.

And I want to thank the chair again for holding this hearing, and I yield back.

Mr. SMITH. Thank you very much, Commissioner Pitts.

Dr. Burgess.

HON. MICHAEL BURGESS, COMMISSIONER, COMMISSION ON SECURITY AND COOPERATION IN EUROPE

Dr. BURGESS. Thank you, Chairman Smith. Thank you for having this hearing.

I'll keep my remarks brief because the numbers have been very well stated by other people on the dais, but we all recognize the conflict in Syria is moving into its fifth year. The Islamic State controls large areas of both Syria and Iraq. And Russia has now intervened militarily on behalf of the Syrian Government, further exacerbating tensions among the armed resistance groups, terrorist insurgents, and those loyal to President Assad.

These factors have contributed and created the staggering number of displaced persons that we are seeing, and at least 710,000 refugees have reached Europe's borders just this year. Syrians are the largest group by nationality. Most of them are hoping to reach Germany, Sweden, France, the United Kingdom, and many ultimately the United States.

I think Chairman Smith said it very, very well when he gave you the breakdown of the numbers. And when you just look at the pictures of the people occupying the rail stations awaiting transport to a different destination, yes you see women, yes you see children, but you see an awful lot of young men of military age who are fleeing. This raises questions in the minds of the constituents I represent back in Texas. Why is this particular subset of the population leaving so quickly, leaving so willingly, sacrificing the safety of their loved ones that they leave behind? Why aren't these individuals defending their country and giving access to women and children, the populations who may be most eligible for exploitation by the Islamic State? Why not give them the opportunity to leave first and to be safe? Are these young men leaving to avoid conscription? Or, worse, are they leaving to carry on the fight in other fronts?

Recently European countries pledged to accept an increased number of Syrian refugees and other asylum seekers. In response, on September 20, Secretary of State John Kerry announced the refugee ceiling in the United States for fiscal year 2016 would be 85,000. Previously, the administration announced the United States would admit at least 10,000 Syrian refugees in fiscal year 2016.

Other reports that have come out have suggested that number could be as high as 100[,000] or even 200,000. And I would just suggest to the State Department the differences and the discrepancies in these numbers are leading to a certain amount of unease for the constituents I represent back in Texas. Given the large and sudden increase in the admittance of refugees from one particular war-torn area, some would-be terrorists are bound to try to exploit any deficiencies that occur within our—within the barriers that are set up to prevent their arrival in this country. And of course, as a member of the Commission but also as a member of Congress,

I have a constitutional obligation to have as my number one goal the defense of my nation, and I must not—I must not—I must not forget that responsibility.

How much authority and control does the administration actually have over this process? And is Europe, the first stop for these refugees, implementing appropriate vetting processes before the individuals are moved elsewhere, particularly to the United States? I don't want to diminish the incredible hardship that these individuals have endured, but we must be certain that we aren't inadvertently admitting members of the Islamic State or other terrorist organizations into our country.

I thank the chairman for convening this hearing and I look forward to the testimony of our witnesses. And I'll yield back.

Mr. SMITH. Thank you very much, Dr. Burgess.

And welcome. The Commission's very pleased to welcome Anne Richard, the Assistant Secretary for the Bureau of Population, Refugees, and Migration. Prior to her appointment, Ms. Richard was the vice president of government relations and advocacy for the International Rescue Committee, or the IRC. She also—and I'll put your full resume and that of all of our witnesses into the record, without objection—but from 1999 to 2001 Ms. Richard was director of the Secretary's Office of Resources, Plans and Policy at the State Department from 1997 to 1999. She was deputy chief financial officer for the Peace Corps. Earlier, she served as a senior adviser in the Deputy Secretary's Office of Public Policy Resources at State and as budget examiner at the U.S. Office of Management and Budget.

Thank you for being here, and the floor is yours.

ANNE C. RICHARD, ASSISTANT SECRETARY, BUREAU OF POPULATION, REFUGEES, AND MIGRATION, U.S. DEPARTMENT OF STATE

Sec. RICHARD. Thank you very much, Chairman Smith. Thank you, members of the Helsinki Commission, for holding this hearing and for the opportunity to appear before you to discuss the refugee and migration emergency in Europe and the Middle East.

I have just returned from a series of meetings overseas, including my fifth visit to Turkey and my eighth visit to Jordan in my tenure as assistant secretary. It's a very challenging situation, and I would like to briefly outline the steps taken by the Population, Refugees, and Migration Bureau and others at the State Department, and U.S. Agency for International Development and in the Obama administration to help provide humanitarian assistance to innocent civilians and to assist the governments of other countries to deal with this crisis.

As you know, in early September the tragic photo of a little boy's body on a beach in Turkey awakened people to the plight of Syrian refugees in ways that years of grim statistics, bleak images and climbing casualties figures could not. What started as unrest in Syria in 2011 has developed into a multi-front war and spilled over to become a regional crisis. And now the crisis has reached Europe as hundreds of thousands of young men, women, and sometimes entire families seek to reach that continent by boat, bus, train, and foot. They are joined by refugees and migrants from other countries, chiefly Afghanistan, Eritrea, and Iraq. They are taking pathways to Europe that migrants have always used, but the scale of this migration is much bigger than before and has caught the attention of the world.

Americans want to understand what is causing the crisis, how we are responding, and what more we can do to help. While there has always been migration to Europe through Africa and across the Mediterranean, the numbers began to rise noticeably in mid-2013. Smugglers took advantage of the breakdown of law and order in Libya to profit from and exploit migrants and refugees desperate to reach Europe. The numbers have grown steadily. So far in 2015 more than 600,000 people have crossed the Mediterranean and Aegean Seas to seek entry into Europe. Some come by boat from Libya to Italy. Others come the Western Balkans route from Turkey by boat to Greece and then onward. As the numbers of migrants have risen, so too have we seen an increase in the number of drownings and death: 3,200 people died in 2014 and more than 3,000 so far this year.

Syrian refugees in Jordan, Turkey, and Lebanon are losing hope of ever returning to their homes. They are worried about the reliability of food and assistance programs that are being reduced for lack of funds, as you mentioned earlier, Mr. Smith. They don't have regular work to sustain their families, rents are high, and their children are missing out on school.

Today an estimated 6.5 million Syrians are internally displaced, and nearly 4.1 million are refugees. More than half of these refugees are children. Along with the so-called push factors—what's going wrong that's pushing them out of the region—there are undeniable pull factors prompting individuals and families to make this trip. These include the summer weather, a perception that Europe was suddenly open to unlimited refugee arrivals, fear that the policy would change without notice and borders would close, and desire to join friends and relatives who had already made it to Europe. It is important for us to remember and acknowledge that the vast majority of Syrian refugee families—96 percent—remain in the Middle East.

The U.S. Government is very much engaged in responding to the crisis and has been for some time. We have a three-pronged approach: Strong levels of humanitarian assistance—and for this we have to thank bipartisan support from the Congress; active diplomacy; and expanded refugee resettlement. The U.S. Government is a leading donor of humanitarian assistance to people in need inside Syria, in the surrounding countries, and to others caught up in crises around the world. Through contributions to international organizations such as the U.N. High Commissioner for Refugees, the International Committee of the Red Cross, the International Organization for Migration, the World Food Programme, UNICEF and leading nongovernmental organizations, U.S. funds are being used to save millions of lives.

On September 21st, the White House announced that the United States will provide nearly 419 million [dollars] in additional assistance for those affected by the war in Syria. That was our last large announcement for that fiscal year, and this brought our total of humanitarian assistance in response to the Syrian conflict to more than 4.5 billion [dollars] since the start of the crisis. Without our support, I believe more people would be making the dangerous voyage further north.

However, even with our sizeable contributions, U.N. appeals for humanitarian aid to address this crisis in Syria remain underfunded. And, Mr. Smith, you presented a lot of those numbers, and you made the completely accurate point that we see that about 60 percent of the response to the appeals for inside Syria and in the surrounding countries goes unfunded, and that's the case across the board with all of the major humanitarian emergencies right now. It's a major frustration. And it's not because the U.S. isn't doing its share. The U.S. is a major funder of all of these humanitarian operations. But even though we're doing more than we've ever done before, it's not enough relative to the need. Contributions from other donor governments, the private sector and the public are urgently needed.

The second prong of our response is diplomacy on humanitarian issues. For several years we have engaged government officials in the region to encourage them to keep borders open, allow refugees to enter their countries, authorize the work of leading humanitarian organizations, and allow refugees to pursue normal life—as normal as possible given what they have been through. We are part of a chorus of nations that call for the respect of humanitarian principles even inside Syria in wartime.

Diplomacy on humanitarian issues means working constructively with other nations to find solutions. The issue of the refugee and migration crisis was taken up again and again in recent international fora such as the U.N. General Assembly in New York in September, the U.N. High Commissioner for Refugees Executive Committee in Geneva in early October, and the just-concluded Global Forum on Migration and Development in Istanbul. All provided opportunities for countries to come together in a common effort. I attended the first and led the U.S. delegation to the others. At all of these venues we met on the sidelines with government officials involved in the crisis, from Sweden and Germany to Lebanon, Jordan, and Turkey.

Diplomacy also includes pushing when needed those who can and should be doing more to do so. Many countries choose to provide assistance outside the U.N. system. However, we are deeply engaged on encouraging other countries to contribute to the U.N. appeals to Syria, to help prevent duplication, ensure that precious and scarce humanitarian assistance is provided to those who need it the most. We are also encouraging countries to identify opportunities for refugees to pursue livelihoods and become more self-sufficient in ways that do not exacerbate existing unemployment issues in host countries.

The third prong of our response is resettling refugees in the United States. Since 1975, the U.S. has welcomed over 3 million refugees from all over the world under the U.S. Refugee Admissions Program. In fiscal year 2015, nearly 70,000 refugees of 67 different nationalities were admitted for permanent resettlement to the United States. This was the third year in a row that we reached our target of 70,000.

So in fiscal year 2016 the President has determined that we should increase that number to 85,000, including at least 10,000 Syrians. And as you know, we would then strive, if successful, to reach 100,000 refugees from around the world in the following year.

We need to continue and expand our efforts. And we seek to work even more closely with the European Union and its member countries, as well as those countries not part of the European Union, to help shape a comprehensive and coordinated response. And we have already started that process.

In the Middle East, we are working on an initiative to get more refugee children in school in Turkey. Education for children who have been displaced, whatever their status and wherever they land, is essential for their own futures and for ours. We support the No Lost Generation campaign to educate and protect Syrian children and youth. Given the protracted nature of this crisis, we are also looking at new ways to better link our relief and development assistance. With roughly 85 percent of refugees now living outside of camps, in cities and villages throughout the Middle East, we need to be working to help refugees become self-sufficient and support the communities that host them.

So, once again, the U.S. must join with enlightened leaders in Europe to take action, and this builds on the work the Obama administration has been doing for more than four years to help the countries neighboring Syria and address the needs of innocent people caught up in the Syria crisis.

I know that it was said that the U.S., Europe and the OSCE are debating what to do. I think Europe is debating, but the U.S. is very much doing. We're doing a lot, and we're seeking to be as helpful as possible. And that is the message that in recent weeks we've been telling European ambassadors and leaders, foreign ministers, prime ministers. And this builds on what we've been saying to the leaders of Lebanon, Jordan, Turkey, Iraq in the previous several years.

So I'm very happy, with that, to answer your questions about my testimony and related issues.

Mr. SMITH. Thank you very much, Madam Secretary. Let me ask first, and I'll throw out a few questions and then yield to my colleagues because we all have many, many questions.

In terms of the number of people potentially going to be resettled here in the United States, the UNHCR suggests that 10 percent of the Syrian refugees, or some 400,000 persons in total, are in need of resettlement. In the testimony that will be provided today, Mr. Pitterman says that UNHCR has already referred more than 45,000 Syrians for refugee resettlement, with more than 20,000 of those referrals made to the United States. Although Syrian arrivals to the U.S. have been fewer than 2,000 persons so far, he notes that they are encouraged by the intent to admit at least 10,000 in fiscal year 2016.

My question is, the 2,000 that have come here, this referral of some 20,000 that have been made, at what state of process of going through their cases, where are we on that? Where are they right now, physically? And with regards to the robust efforts to ensure that ISIS and other potential groups of lone wolves or wolf packs,

groups of individuals who come here with malice on their mind—
I know we have a very robust way of doing our screening. I've
looked at it very carefully. Without objection, a Congressional Research Service—several paragraphs describing that will be made
part of the record, because I think it is robust. But it's very hard
to do a background check on people about which you know very,
very little, and there's very little database available anywhere to
ascertain what their motives might be.

And I'm wondering how we bridge that gap to ensure that we are
not unwittingly welcoming to this country—those like the young
man who came in from Stenkovec during the Kosovo crisis. I'm
sure he wasn't the only one, but it happened right inside of my own
district. And I remember, you know, I was there. Planeloads of people were coming down. People from the community in Mercer
County and Burlington County and Ocean Counties met them with
a great deal of affection, and yet included among them was a man
who would seek to work with the Fort Dix Five to murder service
members and their families at Fort Dix. Thankfully, that plot was
thwarted and they are now in prison—at least the five from the
Fort Dix Five.

So your thoughts on that, and then I have a couple of other questions. Then I'll yield to Commissioner Pitts.

Sec. RICHARD. Well, thank you, Mr. Chairman.

We have brought nearly 2,000 Syrians to the United States as
part of the U.S. Refugee Admissions Program since 2011, and the
numbers have climbed very slowly. Last year we brought—in
2015—1,682, so almost 1,700.

Mr. SMITH. And is that because of vetting issues, or ... ?

Sec. RICHARD. Well, there were a couple of things.

First is that when there is a crisis and people flee, you don't
automatically start a refugee resettlement program because our
hope initially is that they'll be able to go home again. And quite
candidly, in the first year or so of this crisis, I really thought that
it would be over soon and people would be able to go back. So when
that did not become the case, in 2013 UNHCR started to think
about a resettlement program for Syrians who had fled to neighboring countries.

That's where most of the refugees who have been referred to us
are. They are living in the countries that neighbor Syria—the top
four countries are Turkey, Jordan, Lebanon, Iraq, and also some
are as far afield as Egypt. And we already were resettling refugees
from this area because we were resettling Iraqi refugees who had
fled to these countries, including Syria.

So the other reason it takes a while to bring people here is our
process currently takes between an average of 18 to 24 months because refugee applicants have to go through a series of steps. The
most important thing I can say related to security is that no one
comes here who hasn't been approved by the Department of Homeland Security. So no foreign entity or organization is deciding for
us who comes to the United States, who crosses that border.

And as you noted, there have been nearly 22,000 referrals made,
so there are a number of people who the UNHCR has determined
would potentially be good applicants for our program. So who's a
good applicant for our program? Well, we tend to take people who

are particularly vulnerable, people for whom going home to Syria is just not in the cards. It's just likely never to happen again.

So these are people who have been, for example, torture victims, who would be traumatized by returning to what once was their homes. These are people who have lost family members. Sometimes they have suffered bodily harm, families with children that have burns or have been traumatized. People who could benefit from some of the advanced medicines—medical technology that we can provide here. People who need to make a fresh start. And this is in keeping with the way we've been running the program for some years.

And the amazing thing is that these people—who are among the most vulnerable—turn out to make perfectly fine residents in the United States and often are able to come back, to support themselves. The kids to extremely well in school and they go on to thrive. We've seen this with so many communities over the years. So I'm fairly confident that this will be the case for Syrian refugees.

In terms of the security process, the refugees have helped putting together their story—a case file on who they are, why they had to flee, and what their own personal histories are. And this is either an individual or a family will have a case. And then we have organizations that we fund in the Middle East to help them put that story together and then be prepared for an interview by a Department of Homeland Security interviewer.

The interviewers from DHS are very well trained, so that even if there is not a lot of existing information about these individuals in U.S. files, they can see whether their stories hold up, whether they were at the right place at the right time—they can look at their documents. They can sort out what's been forged and what's actually authentic. They take their time on these interviews. They're very patient. I've sat in on some of the interviews. Now, I mean, maybe they had me sit in one of the ones that were particularly well run, but still I came away very impressed by how our DHS colleagues walked very carefully through these stories, and double check and recheck. And then they also run the names against the national security and law enforcement databases that the United States maintains. And essentially, we're weeding out people who are liars, who are criminals, or who are would-be terrorists. And so this is partly why of the 3 million people we've brought here, we have very few cases of people ending up getting into trouble or threatening trouble.

That doesn't mean that we should let our guard down. I think we can only run this program taking every possible step to keep out bad guys. I completely agree with that, and I know the entire State Department agrees with me on this. [Chuckles.] But we have to do both. We have to run a program that is as efficient as possible, that provides a humanitarian pathway to a new life for a number of the refugees, and we have to keep out the people who are up to no good.

Mr. SMITH. Just a few final questions.

We know what the amount of money unmet—the unmet need that's not being provided by the international community in percentage terms. What is it in actual dollar terms—what is the unmet need for this crisis?

Secondly, are you considering the designation of any P–2 groups for Syrians, including Christians and other minority religions? Is that under active consideration?

And on the trafficking issue, there have been a number of reports—as you know, I'm the author of the Trafficking Victims Protection Act and I'm the special representative for the OSCE Parliamentary Assembly on trafficking. And we know it's a huge problem in the United States, in Europe, around the world, but it's often exploited by traffickers during refugee situations or war situations, and this obviously is both. We've heard reports that in places like Bavaria—there's one refugee camp there where one worker described it at the biggest brothel in Munich and pointed out that, again, women—80 percent of the camp residents are men, and the women have a very, very risky life just living there, and they are trafficked and exploited and raped. And I'm wondering if you believe enough is being done in Europe to ensure that this kind of exploitation of women does not occur, and whether or not our TIP Office is actually working and collaborating with people in Europe, who I know personally care deeply about the trafficking issue.

And then I'll yield to Mr. Pitts.

Sec. RICHARD. The first question was about the funding. The second question, can you just remind me?

Mr. SMITH. Was about the P–2.

Sec. RICHARD. Oh, right, the P–2 category.

Mr. SMITH. Whether or not you are actively considering designating Christians and Yazidis and other minority religions as P–2 category for immigration purposes, to bring these folks over.

Sec. RICHARD. The appeal for last year for both inside Syria and around Syria was around $8 billion, and I believe that it was funded at about—we're looking at 4 or 5 [billion dollars]. It's on a calendar-year basis, so we'll see how much is brought in by the end of December. But most of the funding, I think, has been provided.

On the P–2, the advantage of a P–2 category is that it helps UNHCR—it helps us get referrals. It facilitates that. Since we have 22,000 referrals right now, it's not a problem for us. So it's not something that would benefit us right at the moment. We can always take a fresh look at that.

But behind your question was a concern about minorities, and certainly we definitely define the vulnerable people to include religious and ethnic minorities. And that includes Christian minorities and the Yazidis in Iraq. Forty percent of the refugees we've brought from Iraq have been Christians or other ethnic or religious minorities.

Now, with the Syrians, I don't think we'll find those large percentages because we just don't have such large percentages in the groups of refugees that have fled the country. So we'll be certainly looking at protections for those groups, but they're not as prevalent in the refugee flows as they have been for Iraqis.

We have heard the stories about the exploitation taking place in Germany. We're very concerned about it. Yes, our Trafficking in Persons Office has been involved in the administration's refugee response. They've been integrated in our response through participation at senior and working levels and working groups focused on migration and refugee flows, as well as law enforcement surrounding human smuggling. We, like you, share our horror at what happens to women and girls when any big migration or refugee flow happens. You know, we have worked hard to agree with the organizations we fund that we shouldn't wait for the evidence, we should just assume bad things are happening and put in place early steps to prevent sexual and gender-based violence.

So I don't have evidence of the specific situation in Germany. We have a very close working relationship right now with the Germans. I accompanied Secretary Kerry when he visited Germany and met with Syrian refugees there and talked to their foreign minister. I met with him in New York. So we can follow up and find out more about——

Mr. SMITH. And I would note that the Munich example is only one of many that we have here. So I'm hoping that the TIP Office is collaborating not just with State, but also with the Europeans?

Sec. RICHARD. I don't know. They're very involved.

Mr. SMITH. OK.

Sec. RICHARD. And so I'll go back and find out——

Mr. SMITH. If you could get back.

Sec. RICHARD. ——to what extent we're tracking down some of these stories because we don't have evidence of the specific things that we've seen on the Web taking place, but I believe bad things could be happening because they always do. And so I think we have to run down these stories working with the German Government.

Mr. SMITH. OK. Thank you.

Sec. RICHARD. And I'm very happy to work with the TIP Office on that.

Mr. SMITH. Commissioner Pitts?

Mr. PITTS. Thank you, Mr. Chairman.

Thank you, Madam Secretary, for coming today. And I want to emphasize that I think you should prioritize Christians and ethnic minorities for the P–2 resettlement program because I think they're most at risk.

But let me go back to this question about all the young men in the refugee flow that Dr. Burgess raised and the type of vetting processes that are utilized before admitting refugees to the United States. I heard you say you review their stories, you check the international criminal database. What other steps do you take to vet these refugees?

Sec. RICHARD. Well, if you want to get in deep into the details, we can have a classified briefing, which we've been giving more often now to members of Congress. And DHS are really the experts on it. But the steps include, then, the referral from UNHCR, so they weed out people who are not appropriate to refer to us; the preparation of their case; very importantly, the interview by DHS examiners; and then checking their names and their biometric data—their fingerprints—against U.S. law enforcement and national security databases. When there's a question, sometimes applicants are put on hold while further investigations are carried out. So nobody comes to the United States about whom there are any open questions. DHS takes their role extremely seriously.

Mr. PITTS. And how long will this vetting process continue? How long does it take?

Sec. RICHARD. Right now the average is 18 to 24 months. There is a sense in the administration this is too long. And part of it is we want it to be as quickly as possible for the sake of the refugees, but we also wanted to make sure we don't cut any corners that would relate to security.

So in the coming months we will be carrying out a review of the program. Senior White House officials have asked us to make sure we bring a fresh set of eyes to this, so we will be working probably to bring in consultants to see if there are ways to speed up the process without cutting certain corners.

Mr. PITTS. Do you ever turn anyone down——

Sec. RICHARD. Turn lots of people down.

Mr. PITTS. ——for a lack of information?

Sec. RICHARD. I have to refer you to DHS on that. But no one comes if they have any question about their safety.

Mr. PITTS. To what degree do European governments share this concern about the potential for Islamic terrorists to exploit the crisis to gain a foothold in Europe?

Sec. RICHARD. Well, they 100 percent share the concern, but they are not in a position to run the kind of program we are, as they have people walking across borders to reach their countries.

I was recently speaking and met the number two from the German embassy here. He said, I wish we had the luxury of taking 18 to 24 months to vet people before they cross our borders.

So we are working to support UNHCR, to help make sure that at the borders as many people possible are screened and registered, and a determination is made, are they bona fide refugees, are they people who are perhaps economic migrants who had just come for a job and are not fleeing persecution. But I think, on this next panel, this is a good question to put to some of the European witnesses, is to get at what they are able to do and what they are unable to do with the flow currently coming from the Middle East.

Mr. PITTS. And where are these individuals held while you're doing this screening? Where are they?

Sec. RICHARD. Some of the refugees are in camps in Turkey—in southern Turkey and in northern Jordan. Many live outside of camps, as I mentioned. So they're living in apartments or in homes, sometimes with relatives. They're living on their own. They come to UNHCR offices to apply for the program, where they're referred by UNHCR or NGO staff who know about their situations and think they might make good candidates for resettlement in a third country.

Mr. PITTS. You know, Secretary Kerry announced that the refugee ceiling in 2017 will be 100,000. What nationalities do you anticipate admitting in significant number next year?

Sec. RICHARD. Well, in the past the three top nationalities were Burmese, Bhutanese, and Iraqis. And that's changing because we've brought so many Bhutanese from Nepal that the numbers are now going down. We will still see significant numbers of Burmese, Iraqis, and Somalis are climbing in terms of their percentage coming. So that will continue to be the case. I think what you'll see is about half of the people coming will be from Africa and half will be—roughly, 40 to 50 percent—from the Middle East.

Mr. PITTS. And what are the most common root causes for displacement in Africa?

Sec. RICHARD. Well, in terms of becoming a refugee, you have to prove that you're fleeing—you have a well-founded fear of persecution for one of five reasons, which are race, nationality, religion, political belief, or membership in a particular social group.

Displacement in Africa, of course, happens for more than that reason. Some people are fleeing famine. Some people are fleeing at one point Ebola. But right now we see big displacement because of poor governance and fighting in South Sudan. People have been living outside of Somalia in nearby countries for years now as that government—first for the violence, and now as that government tries to get its feet under it. We're seeing more and more people coming from West Africa who are fleeing Boko Haram in northern Nigeria, and they're going to several countries nearby. We also have unrest in Burundi causing people to flee. So often it's governance—poor governance, fighting.

Mr. PITTS. You haven't mentioned Syria yet. How many Syrian refugee cases has UNHCR referred to the U.S. program?

Sec. RICHARD. It's about 22,000 now.

Mr. PITTS. Twenty-two thousand. And at what stage are these cases in the U.S. resettlement consideration process?

Sec. RICHARD. They're at all stages of the process. Because it takes a couple of years, we are only just now seeing large numbers arrive. And so that's why we're anticipating that this year we can climb from nearly—let me see—nearly 1,700 last year to more like 10,000 this year.

Mr. PITTS. OK. And where will the United States process Syrian refugee cases this year?

Sec. RICHARD. So the top places will be in Jordan—in Amman, Jordan and in Turkey. And we also have some other facilities in the region. We would like to start bringing people out of Lebanon, but we're delayed doing that at the moment. So let's see. So Jordan is number one. Turkey, Egypt are the other countries where we can bring sizeable numbers right now.

Mr. PITTS. OK. All right.

Finally, OSCE. Could you elaborate on the role that OSCE could have in monitoring the treatment of refugees as they transit from OSCE countries?

Sec. RICHARD. I'd like to answer that question. Before I do, I would just say—because I didn't know this until I saw it on the piece of paper in front of me—[laughs]—that of 18,000 referrals we have right now, 4,000 have been interviewed by DHS already and 14,000 are awaiting their interview or getting ready for their interview.

On the OSCE, we welcome any efforts by the Organization for Security and Cooperation in Europe and any of its institutions or field missions to coordinate with UNHCR and other international organizations to provide assistance to countries dealing with refugee and migration crises in Europe. The OSCE Secretariat and institutions such as the Office for Democratic Institutions and

Human Rights and the High Commissioner for National Minorities have experience helping countries respond to crises.

The OSCE has a history of working with UNHCR. Just last year, the OSCE and UNHCR issued a detailed protection checklist outlining the types of actions the two organizations could take in response to various types of crises.

OSCE is hosting a conference in Amman, Jordan with its Mediterranean country partners—so that's Algeria, Egypt, Israel, Jordan, Morocco, Tunisia—today and tomorrow to discuss common challenges to European security, including the irregular migration, refugee protection and trafficking in persons concerns. And of course we support efforts by OSCE in this regard, and U.S. Ambassador to the OSCE Daniel Baer is leading the U.S. delegation to the conference.

We also believe that OSCE will be putting together an appeal for some funding from us, and so that our Euro colleagues would be taking a look at funding that.

Mr. PITTS. Thank you, Madam Secretary.

Thank you, Mr. Chairman.

Mr. SMITH. Thank you.

Commissioner Shaheen.

HON. JEANNE SHAHEEN, COMMISSIONER, COMMISSION ON SECURITY AND COOPERATION IN EUROPE

Ms. SHAHEEN. Thank you very much.

I just returned with three other senators from a trip to Europe. We visited Greece, the island of Lesbos, where many refugees are coming in, and then we visited Germany. And one of the things that we heard from all the officials that we talked with—again, we met with some officials from Frontex, from UNHCR, people at reception centers who are dealing with the crisis—was that they hoped that the United States would be able to do more to help.

So you've talked a little bit about some of the challenges that we have in terms of vetting refugees, but can you elaborate a little bit on the obstacles to bringing refugees in, and then also to the challenge of providing humanitarian assistance? I know that the United States is one of the top countries in terms of providing humanitarian assistance, but my understanding is that the U.N. appeal is only 41 percent funded. And are there other ways in which we can urge countries to be more supportive of those humanitarian efforts?

Sec. RICHARD. Thank you for your trip to the region, which I heard about when I was in Turkey. And I'll be very interested to hear how——

Ms. SHAHEEN. We learned a lot.

Sec. RICHARD. I know I answer the questions, but I'm still curious to hear how your—[chuckles]—your trip went.

The challenges of bringing refugees in is that we want to be certain we're bringing the right people.

Ms. SHAHEEN. Sure.

Sec. RICHARD. And so getting this balance right between determining who the most vulnerable are, who are the people who would benefit the most from restarting their lives in the United States, and also ensuring that our security measures are good so that we keep out anyone with bad intentions, that's the tricky thing to do. And it involves several U.S. Government agencies, it involves a couple of major international organizations, and it involves many not-for-profit nongovernmental organizations on both sides of the ocean. So there are many hands that help the refugees along the way, and that takes time.

The good part is that it's a very successful program that works year in and year out. We've brought 70,000 refugees to the United States from all around the world over the past three years. I meet refugees all around the United States and I ask them is this a good program? Should we continue to run it? And they feel it is a life-saving program that has given their whole family a chance for a new future. And personally, I feel that it strengthens the United States to have such diverse population and be bringing in people from all around the world, and that it adds to our culture, our fabric. So I am convinced that the program should continue and should be strong, and will likely be strong. But it does take a lot of steps, and it's also a public-private partnership.

The life of a refugee coming to the United States is very challenging. It is not a luxurious program. Within one to three months of arriving, able-bodied refugees have to get a job. And many refugees, if they don't speak English well, they have to start over at the bottom of the economic ladder. But they do it, and employers tell us that they're very, very good, highly motivated workers. Children get enrolled in school. The younger the kids are, the more quickly they adapt. Older kids takes a little longer. But generally, the program's great.

Ms. SHAHEEN. Sure. And I'm sorry to interrupt, but I actually support our program. The question that I'm really asking is, are there ways for us to be more efficient—do the same kind of vetting, but to do it in a way that is more efficient, that better coordinates all the various players who are part of the effort so that we can more effectively respond when we see this kind of a crisis?

Sec. RICHARD. The process has had a lot of scrutiny from the National Security Council and the White House over the course of this administration. And so a lot of steps have been taken—a lot of sort of the easier steps have been taken to tighten up the program, but my sense is that few of us are satisfied that it still takes an average of 18 to 24 months to bring people.

So we've been asked to take a fresh look, and in the coming months to have consultants come in and review the whole process and see if we can shorten the time span that it takes to bring refugees without cutting corners on security.

Ms. SHAHEEN. Thank you. And can you respond on the 41 percent of funding that's actually been produced for humanitarian efforts? And if you could also speak to some of our allies in the Middle East, in Arab countries, and their commitment to help with refugees.

Sec. RICHARD. So even though we're providing sort of what I see as the foundation of the humanitarian assistance that goes to some of the, you know, most effective operational organizations overseas, and we get very solid support—bipartisan support—from the House and the Senate, it's not enough funding. And so we need other countries to provide assistance and other countries to do more.

So first the traditional donors may have been suffering from fatigue, because I felt in the last year or two that their contributions, while increasing, were not keeping pace with the needed increases. So certainly Europe now is very focused on needing to provide more assistance to help the refugees who are in the Middle East and are displaced inside Syria, and also refugees in the surrounding—neighboring countries.

Then, for a couple of years now, we have been trying to encourage Gulf States to become routine, regular donors to and through United Nations appeals, and I would say we've had mixed success on this. We have seen some very large, generous contributions, but they tend to be one-time-only checks written. They're not always through the U.N. They're nothing you can count on will happen again the following year.

We're very appreciative that Kuwait held three annual pledging conferences on the Syria crisis, and I attended all of them. That did help to put real money on the table, and the U.S. and Kuwait were the top donors in response to those pledging conferences. But it's not enough, and we what we'd like to see is some more Gulf States become regular, annual donors in a dependable way with the United Nations.

Then we look at the U.S. and the U.K. and France as part of the permanent five members of the U.N. Security Council. But Russia and China are also members, and we don't see them being engaged on humanitarian activities—supporting humanitarian activities to the way that the other members are. So we would like to see more countries involved and joining the table of traditional donors, expand that.

Then we also are very interested in getting more private-sector contributions from philanthropies, foundations, but also businesses and from the public. So for me, it's been very gratifying that in recent weeks we have seen that happen. And we've gone from wondering how to make that happen to seeing it really happen. Now the question is, how can we make this a sustaining interest?

What we've seen is that Americans can be very generous, but tend to prefer to give after natural disasters—like the earthquake in Haiti, I believe half of all households were reported—Americans households were reported to give. So I think there's been a sense that the situation in the Middle East is messy and there's a lot of bad guys running around, and we didn't want to do anything to support them. But I know that there are a lot of families—innocent families—who are being victimized by terrorists who deserve help. And I think when Americans see the faces of these families, they realize, oh, these are people we have to help, we must help, we feel compelled to help. So I'd like to build on some of the generosity that we've seen in recent weeks. And of course, this is not the responsibility of the U.S. Government to do that, but to encourage it certainly and see more giving from more private sector and more members of the public.

Ms. SHAHEEN. Thank you.

Thank you, Mr. Chairman. I have other questions, but I'll reserve them for the next panel.

Mr. SMITH. Thank you.

Dr. Burgess.

Dr. BURGESS. Thank you, Mr. Chairman.

And thank you, Madam Secretary, for being here today.

You said in your opening statement that one of the drivers of the flood of refugees to Europe was the perception that Europe was open. Can you expand upon that a little bit? What gave people that impression?

Sec. RICHARD. I think that the fact that early waves were getting all the way to Germany and were being received in Germany, then may have, through social media and through just plain old media, suggested to people this is the time to go and that they would be able to make it all the way. It's probably a best question answered by Europeans, but without being an expert on all the specific details on this, I think that that was part of what was happening.

Dr. BURGESS. Well, you mentioned social media, and that was actually what I was going to get to. Was social media one of the drivers that led to this?

Sec. RICHARD. I've been told that you can get a lot of information about how to make the voyage—[chuckles]—and the journey off of the Web and off of one's phone.

Dr. BURGESS. I would expect that that's probably true.

As far as the 1,700 individuals that were approved in that—this last fiscal year, fiscal year 2016?

Sec. RICHARD. They arrived.

Dr. BURGESS. They arrived. And those all went through the DHS vetting process? And of that 1,700, how many were not approved? And what then happened to them?

Sec. RICHARD. No, the 1,700 is the number that were approved. So I don't have the numbers that were disapproved or rejected to come, and we can try to get that for you.

Dr. BURGESS. And then the numbers are going to go up, so there is going to be a scaling issue with Department of Homeland Security being able to keep up with the numbers that you will be asking them to vet. Is that correct?

Sec. RICHARD. That is very correct.

Dr. BURGESS. And what are the discussions that you've had with the secretary of homeland security or that Secretary Kerry has had with the secretary of homeland security about what you're doing in your agency and what they might expect in their agency?

Sec. RICHARD. We have had a series, for a couple years now, of interagency meetings that the NSC has pulled together and deputies committee meetings and even a principals committee meeting or two, so at different levels of the executive branch, that bring together the State Department, Health and Human Services—because they provide assistance to the states to help——

Dr. BURGESS. Yeah, I have some questions I want to ask you about that. But yeah, go on.

Sec. RICHARD. ——[chuckles]—after refugees get here—and then DHS and also some of the other law enforcement and national security agencies to make sure all of these pieces are working together. And there is a lot of pressure now for DHS to get more interviewers hired, trained and out to the field so that they can support bringing higher numbers of refugees—out to the field all around the world, and not just in the Middle East.

Dr. BURGESS. Certainly in Texas last summer—July of 2014—we saw some of the deficiencies of the Office of Refugee Relocation through the Department of Health and Human Services, who were responsible for processing and handing the unaccompanied minors as they came through, and it seemed like they were pretty much at or beyond their limit. Are you talking with your counterparts in the Department of Health and Human Services about additional stresses that may be placed on their system because of the numbers that you're bringing—proposing to bring in?

Sec. RICHARD. So all of the agencies—all three of the agencies that play the biggest roles in this have to make tradeoffs in terms of their budgets about what they're going to fund related to this program. So for the State Department, the question is how much of our funding goes to overseas assistance to help people who are either displaced in their own countries or refugees nearby, and how much do we then spend to bring refugees to the United States? And right now we're spending about $400 million of our budget for them. So most of our funding goes overseas, but it is sizeable.

Then, for DHS, the question was, do they use their staff to help asylum applicants in the United States or do they send them overseas to do these interviews? And the two missions were competing against each other to a certain extent over the past year. So hiring more interviewers will help address that issue.

And then the Office of Refugee Resettlement in HHS has a couple of different responsibilities. And as you rightly point out, one of them is to help unaccompanied minor children arriving in the United States, such as happened last summer—and has happened since, but it peaked last summer at the U.S.-Mexico border. And so they are responsible for these unaccompanied minor children, but they also are responsible for providing assistance through the states to help refugees beyond that initial three months' reception and placement piece that the State Department funds, for special programs either to help people who need a little longer time getting a job or with English-language classes or other special programs.

So all of these things cost money. And right now the administration is looking, working with OMB, to determine if we need to be requesting increases in our budgets to handle these things. But I think your question is right on target in terms of where we need to be doing more work in providing answers to you.

Dr. BURGESS. Well, and of course it's not your agency, but ORR specifically, in my opinion, needs to work more closely with the states that are going to be affected by the people who are then resettled in those communities. There are stresses that are placed upon our local governments, our school districts, because of the numbers of people who are resettled in those communities.

Sec. RICHARD. I think that is my responsibility, though, as someone who's got the whole——

Dr. BURGESS. I had this discussion with Secretary Nuland when she came before us a year and a half ago. Yes, I think it would be good if State would talk to perhaps senators or even individual members of Congress about people who are being resettled within their district boundaries or their state boundaries. I think that would be extremely helpful. My personal experience has been that does not happen. I've not been as affected as some other members of Congress and other senators, but it certainly does occur. It's something you hear about from your local folks all the time.

Sec. RICHARD. It's a requirement of the program, and we have made it more specific what has to be done, that the nine groups that resettle refugees in the United States with us—they're all not-for-profit; six are faith-based, three are not—that they consult with community leaders about their plans for resettling refugees so that the local sheriff and the mayor and the school superintendent are not surprised when people are showing up in their villages, in their homes, in their cities.

I recently, at the end of August, traveled to Spartanburg, South Carolina, because Congressman Trey Gowdy had questions about whether sufficient consultation was done. And so I went down and traveled with his staff and met with a lot of local leaders there. So I see this as part of our job to make sure that this happens.

I'm sorry, I can't get to better know a district in all—[laughs]—435, but we are making——

Dr. BURGESS. But you know where the people are going. I mean, it's not a surprise to you.

Sec. RICHARD. Texas is number one; 7,479 refugees went to Texas last year. I'm sure a lot of refugees would like to live in Texas.

But so what we're doing is we're making sure that it's a requirement of our partners that do the actual reception and placement that they check with local leaders and they do it four times a year.

Dr. BURGESS. Perhaps if you could provide me some of that data that's been generated by that requirement and divulging that information.

Just before—and I'm going to conclude, but Chairman Smith made the observation about the number of refugees that were young males. Chairman Pitts asked you a similar sort of question. Really, give us some comfort here. When you look at those pictures—and they do seem to be predominantly military-age males with very few women and children scattered throughout—Chairman Smith has some statistics; I think Chairman Pitts had some statistics—why is that? Are these young men fleeing conscription? Is there a—perhaps a darker purpose afoot? Why does it appear that way?

Sec. RICHARD. I think that, for young men coming directly out of Syria, part of it is they are trying to avoid serving in the Assad regime's military, and they do not want to be part of his war effort, and they are people who prefer to live in peace and just want a normal life.

And then, for those fleeing from nearby countries—or not fleeing, but leaving, choosing to leave nearby countries—it's partly because they don't have jobs that are legal jobs. Many are working, but they're working in an underground economy where they can be exploited and abused and underpaid, and that's not appreciated by their neighbors. And so they're looking for a place they can go where they can finish their education, some of them, or they can get their kids in school, because a lot of children are out of school from the Syrian refugee community. And they can acquire skills or practice the professions that they've acquired. And so they're moving to Europe because they think they will have a better life than the places that they've been.

Dr. BURGESS. I guess what I don't understand is why are they leaving and not giving preference to their wives or girlfriends or mothers, people who might be more readily exploitable by ISIS?

Sec. RICHARD. Well, I think that they're leaving their families in places that they believe are safe. Those members of the family inside Syria would not be recruited into the military. I am amazed that nearly 7 million displaced Syrians have stayed inside Syria, though. Part of that is because of programs to try to get as much aid into the country to benefit innocent people as possible. But for the people who are leaving from Turkey and from Jordan, they feel their families are safe. They have achieved safety, but they're not able to afford to live there.

I talked to a woman in Germany who'd left two daughters behind and gone on this dangerous trip by boat from Turkey to Greece with a 5-year-old. And I said, wasn't it dangerous? And she said, yeah, but she could not afford to live in Turkey because the rents were so high. And so she felt that the best thing for the family was to go on ahead, reach Germany, establish a toehold there, and then later send for other family members, or send money back to the older daughters.

I just think these are people who feel very desperate and are taking risks with their families—the kind of risks that we don't have to do in a normal day in the United States. But it's not because they're a threat to the Europeans, it's because they really are looking for opportunity and trying to have a sense that there's hope—they can have hope for a better life.

Dr. BURGESS. Well, I pray that you're right.

Thank you, Mr. Chairman. You've been very indulgent. I'll yield back.

Mr. SMITH. Thank you, Dr. Burgess.

Dr. Boozman.

HON. JOHN BOOZMAN, COMMISSIONER, COMMISSION ON SECURITY AND COOPERATION IN EUROPE

Mr. BOOZMAN. Thank you, Mr. Chairman.

Thank you for being here. We appreciate your hard work.

There's some confusion about what the Gulf States are doing. Can you elaborate on that—what they're doing in regard to the numbers that they're accepting as far as Syrian refugees?

Sec. RICHARD. They're not accepting Syrian refugees. They are giving work visas——

Mr. BOOZMAN. Because Saudi Arabia——

Sec. RICHARD. ——to Syrians to come work in their countries, which is helping some families get out of harm's way and to support themselves.

Mr. BOOZMAN. So that's where the claim of Saudi Arabia that they've got a couple million——

Sec. RICHARD. They have a lot of Syrians living there right now who are working in jobs and have work visas. So that's a good thing for those families. If they lose their jobs, will they have to leave the country? That would be a question I would want to ask.

But what we would like to see is more countries be open to resettling refugees the way we do. And right now, the U.S. is the world leader in doing that. And traditionally, Canada, Australia, the U.K.

and New Zealand are the other countries that take numbers of refugees—sizeable numbers of refugees. So part of our mission is to encourage countries to do more, and what we're seeing is some of their own publics are looking for that now, are asking for that. And what Europe is doing is looking into having that as part of a package of things they'll do to deal with the stream of people headed their way.

Mr. BOOZMAN. What are the top three or four things that the Europeans—what are their top three or four problems that they've got as they manage the crisis?

Sec. RICHARD. The biggest issue is that Europe has a common border now, the EU does, but it's a very porous border in terms of Italy and Greece and the coastline. Different countries have different abilities to manage and secure their borders, and to vet people coming across. And then there are different policies, not only from country to country but also sometimes within a country, for vetting refugees and determining who can stay.

So I believe you're going to be hearing from, in the second panel, some European leaders, so it's probably best for them to describe that. But that's my thumbnail impression of what the problem is right now.

Mr. BOOZMAN. You mentioned the borders. Are there any other policies that you feel like are driving the ability to get into Europe? Does that make sense, any of the European policies that perhaps are driving——

Sec. RICHARD. Well, I think Europeans would say it's not just a question of entering Greece; it's also leaving Turkey and is there a coast guard there? That's one of the things that's being discussed as part of the EU negotiations with Turkey about what else can be done? So——

Mr. BOOZMAN. In line with Congressman Burgess, among those involved in the mixed migration crisis in Europe, what percentage—and again, and also this would pertain to us, but what percentage who are seeking asylum are estimated to be migrants, and the countries involved there, as opposed to what percentage are estimated to be refugees and from which countries?

Sec. RICHARD. I probably have this in this enormous book in front of me. The——

Mr. BOOZMAN. The scenario that you described earlier, with people in regard to the young—the young man coming—you mentioned jobs, things like that. So that would be more migrant than refugee——

Sec. RICHARD. Senator Boozman——

Mr. BOOZMAN. ——would be migrant versus refugee.

Sec. RICHARD. So if you look at these pie charts down here, the dark pink area are people who are considered refugees—recognized as refugees based on those coming, and then the lighter pink is those who have been determined to not qualify as refugees. So it starts to give you a picture that on the Western Balkans route certainly most are fleeing war—are Syrians, Iraqis, Afghanis—or violence. Eritreans are fleeing a repressive government and forced conscription into their national service.

For other parts of Africa it's less refugees and more economic migrants, but for Nigerians, for example, some would be refugees if they're fleeing Boko Haram in Northern Nigeria.

Mr. BOOZMAN. Thank you, Mr. Chairman.

Thank you, Ms. Richard.

Mr. SMITH. Thank you, Senator Boozman.

Commissioner Hultgren?

HON. RANDY HULTGREN, COMMISSIONER, COMMISSION ON SECURITY AND COOPERATION IN EUROPE

Mr. HULTGREN. Thank you so much for your work. Thank you for being here today. And many of my questions and concerns have been discussed already, but I haven't heard you talk much about reaction of local populations in Europe and concern of how they're responding to this significant impact on their countries as far as political parties or some upheaval reacting to the changes that are coming to their countries because of this in certain regions, maybe having significant numbers of refugees there.

From the State Department, what are you sensing there? What concern do you have? And what can we do maybe to help ease some of that fear or uncertainty or the process that they're working through there with this great influx of refugees?

Sec. RICHARD. Well, I think you see European publics responding in a number of ways. Some are quite welcoming to the refugees and some of them are not welcoming at all. And there is a lot of attention to the rise of parties that are xenophobic or anti-immigrant, anti-refugee in various countries of Western Europe. So I'll leave it to European witnesses to discuss that.

I think what the U.S. can do that we are doing is invite people to come here and see how our refugee resettlement program works, because even though it's, like I say, not a luxurious program—it's a public/private partnership that relies on a lot of contributions at the local level in terms of used furniture, used clothing, winter coats for people coming from Somalia to Minnesota—it is one that works.

And so we're trying to sort of model how you can bring people from other cultures, other countries, other religions to your country and all get along just fine. And so that's, I think, the most important thing we can do.

Mr. HULTGREN. We've seen some—I represent Illinois west of Chicago, and World Relief and some other agencies have been fabulous of helping that transition, but I do know—thank you again for your work. I'm going to yield back. I know we've got another panel that we want to hear from as well. So thank you very much, Secretary.

Mr. SMITH. Thank you, sir.

Sec. RICHARD. Thank you.

Mr. SMITH. I want to ask a couple of follow-up questions and then we'll conclude, although we have another member who just joined us.

Let me just ask, how was the 10,000 number arrived at? Why not 15,000? Why not 20[,000]? Why not 5[,000]? Was it scientifically arrived at? Is it a sense that this is our number? Who calculated that number to get to 10,000?

Secondly, EU Ambassador David O'Sullivan will be testifying shortly before this Commission and lays out a number of things that the Europeans have done and continue to do, dozens of initiatives including funding, like us, to UNHCR and other initiatives, but he also points out that we've launched rescuing operations Poseidon and Trident, and tripled our presence at sea. Over 122,000 lives have been saved.

Now, the Sixth Fleet obviously is deployed. There's 26 countries of Europe that are part of that effort—Trident, for example. Are we collaborating? Is the Sixth Fleet collaborating with those rescue efforts at sea? What is our role there?

And finally, Mr. Pitterman makes a very good point talking about long-term trends. Two of them he notes. Why now? Why are people leaving and coming to Europe and potentially to the United States? He said they've lost hope in a political solution to the war, and then after so many years the next resources have run out, living conditions have so deteriorated, two long-term trends, but he said the trigger is the humanitarian funding shortfall—again, the WFP, the World Food Programme's cut of 30 percent that have just driven people to the point where they don't have food so they uproot and leave even their meager existence there. Is that true? Do you agree with that assessment?

Sec. RICHARD. On the second question first, I do think that the cuts in the World Food Program rations and the food voucher values did send a signal, not from the United States, but it was interpreted as a signal from the world that the international community was losing interest and things were going to get harder for refugees in these countries.

So I think many of us feel if we could go back in time that there would have been much more investment in that. And like I say, the U.S. is the leading donor to the World Food Program. So this is not the fault of the United States, but it is a fault of the collective international community that that was allowed to happen. Was it the one single trigger? I don't know. I mean, we've talked about push-and-pull factors, but I think it was a factor, definitely.

Last December, the U.N. High Commissioner for Refugees had a very interesting dialogue. He organized a sort of a more informal meeting every December on a concern, a protection concern, and this past year it was protection at sea. So I asked the U.S. Coast Guard to come along with us to that discussion in Geneva, which doesn't usually happen that we have a joint our bureau with Coast Guard discussion, but I thought that they are so thoughtful in how they do things in the Caribbean that it would be useful for them to be part of the discussion. And also, there were members of the Italian navy who also came. So it was a really unusual meeting where we had nongovernmental organizations, governments, and then coast guards and navies present.

I know that U.S. Navy, U.S. Coast Guard make a priority of saving lives no matter who is approaching their ship and who's in distress nearby. So I'm sure, without knowing the details, that the Sixth Fleet plays a life-saving role in the Mediterranean, but I'm not the expert on how they're working with the European efforts. And so I'll leave that to the next panel.

Mr. SMITH. Again, the 10,000 number? How was that arrived at? And if you could get back to us on the Sixth Fleet I think it would be——

Sec. RICHARD. OK.

Mr. SMITH.——very helpful to the Commission to know. And I know that they would never pass someone who is in distress——

Sec. RICHARD. Sure.

Mr. SMITH.——but are they working with these two European Union efforts?

Sec. RICHARD. On the 10,000 number, we were already planning to increase our numbers to between 5[,000] to 8,000, and the president decided we'd bring a few more than that. So that's how the 10,000 number was arrived at.

Mr. SMITH. We're joined by Commissioner Cohen.

HON. STEVE COHEN, COMMISSIONER, COMMISSION ON SECURITY AND COOPERATION IN EUROPE

Mr. COHEN. Thank you. Thank you, Mr. Chair. First I want to thank you for holding this hearing. It's such an important issue, and so important that America do what America has done so many times in the past, to offer our shores as a place of refuge to people who have been endangered by political conditions in their countries. And I think back personally, as a Jewish American, to the situation with Jews who were not accepted in this country on ships during the 1940s and maybe the 1930s, and I'm sure they met a disastrous outcome because we didn't open our shores at the time. And we should learn from those mistakes, and I believe we will.

I hope that the President will allow for a parole relationship and bring in the refugees who have been cleared who are not in any way—because of the best that we can ascertain—a threat to our country but are in need of refugee status. And I think it's part of what makes our country great and what makes our country the greatest country on the face of the Earth. And as the Pope reminded us, we were all immigrants. The only people that weren't immigrants were victims of one of the greatest slaughters ever, the American Natives, the American Indians.

So, as immigrants, we need to remember, as the Pope told us, the Golden Rule and do unto others as you would have them do unto you. And as I think about possibly my ancestors who would have been on those ships to St. Louis that were not accepted, I think we need to be the great country we are and accept as many folks as we can and save them from the ravages of ISIS and the terrors of war that exist in Syria.

The food program was cut back, as I understand it. Was there any issue with funding for the food program?

Sec. RICHARD. Yes. The Food for Peace Office at the U.S. Agency for International Development leads the U.S. Government in relations with the World Food Program. The World Food Program is headed by an American, Ertharin Cousin from Chicago, and their headquarters is in Rome. We have a very close relationship with them also because sometimes our budget is used when there are food pipeline breaks in terms of the pipeline of food reaching refugees in hard-to-reach places, primarily in Africa.

So the U.S. is the top donor to the World Food Programme year in and year out. It's something I think we're very proud of as Americans, that we don't want people going hungry, but other countries were not keeping up, keeping pace with their contributions as we were. And it wasn't enough for the people running the program in the region to continue to provide benefits to as many refugees as they would have liked.

So what they did was they targeted the most vulnerable, neediest refugees and they cut back then both in the number of people they were reaching and the value of the food vouchers they were giving them. And as we were just discussing, it may have been a trigger for people deciding to leave the region and try to make it to Europe.

Mr. COHEN. In which countries—was the American—our contribution remained constant, is that correct, or was there a cut in funding on our side?

Sec. RICHARD. It's not a cut in funding on our side because both the humanitarian assistance that USAID gets through the Food for Peace program and the Office of Foreign Disaster Assistance, and our budget, have been well-funded by Congress in the last several years. And so one of my messages today is thank you very much, because we are the world leader in providing this humanitarian assistance. And right now we have about $3 billion and AID has about $3 billion in food and disaster assistance that together makes a $6 billion contribution—which is sizable—to needs around the world.

The problem is the list of crises is growing. The old crises continue even as new ones erupt. You know, we're praying that there will be peace in South Sudan, potentially peace in Yemen, places where there have been efforts to resolve conflicts will happen so that we can then use our precious resources for these very, very challenging situations.

Mr. COHEN. Were there other countries that cut back on their financial contribution? And if there were——

Sec. RICHARD. I don't have the details for you, but my sense was they either cut back or they weren't keeping pace with the growth, which we were able to do thanks to Congress.

Mr. COHEN. And which countries were those?

Sec. RICHARD. Well, we were talking before. There is a group of traditional donors, which are Western Europe, U.S., Canada, Korea, Japan, Australia, New Zealand. And so collectively we were unable to keep pace, but I think the U.S. did its share.

Then there's the Gulf States, where sometimes some of them are charitable, particularly charitable and write big checks, and sometimes not. And they tend to give in very one-off situations. And so we would like to see more uniform giving, routine giving from the Gulf States.

And then there are other countries that just do not make a habit of providing assistance through humanitarian assistance. They prefer to do other ways of engaging with the world. I mentioned China and Russia before as to countries that are on the permanent five of the U.N. Security Council, but they're not really part of the traditional donors.

28

Mr. COHEN. Is what you're telling me, and it sounds like it's probably an obvious answer, but the democracies seemed to do pretty good in caring for other people, and the totalitarian regimes and dictatorships don't. So it kind of flows from what they give their own they don't give to others either.

Sec. RICHARD. Well, it's called Western donors, but now we see Japan, Korea. Korea has become a regular donor and didn't used to be. I mean, at one point it was an aid recipient. So I don't think it has to be a Western enterprise. I think that it can be much more internationalized.

Mr. COHEN. But they're all democracies that you say are keeping up with it, Western Europe, Korea, Japan, the United States, Canada, it's the democracies. So that's a good thing.

Sec. RICHARD. Well, and part of it may be that publics expect this from their governments in democracies and make it known that they want to see this happen. You know, the Gulf States can be very charitable. Giving during Ramadan especially goes up. It's a traditional practice in Muslim societies. But it's just not something that right now is part of an annual contribution that can be relied on by U.N. leaders.

Mr. COHEN. Maybe Ramadan should be every day of the week, like Christmas.

Sec. RICHARD. [Chuckles.] And Christmas.

Mr. COHEN. Yeah, exactly, exactly. Who are the people that are— I know Jimmy McGovern's big on feeding the world. Where Jimmy's a leader, is Chris a leader? Who are the leaders in Congress on this?

Sec. RICHARD. How many times do you think I've testified before you, Mr. Smith? I mean, he's very used to it. He's very interested in our issues. So yeah, he's definitely a leader. I met Senator Boozman before and we had a talk about the Syrian refugees. It was after you went I think to Turkey or something. There's been a lot of visitors to Turkey and Jordan, which I find very good in terms of helping me explain to others what is going on.

And then Senator Shaheen just came back from Greece. I haven't been to Greece lately, I would have liked to have gone to Greece. I've got other countries to go to. But it really helps us when you all travel and go out and meet refugees. But one doesn't have to go overseas to meet refugees, of course. There are a lot of refugee families in the United States who can talk about, probably in this room behind me, who can talk about the experiences they've had and what their relatives are going through.

Mr. COHEN. Thank you for your good work.

And thank you, Chairman Smith, for your good work as well.

Mr. SMITH. Thank you very much, Commissioner Cohen.

I'd like to thank you, Madam Secretary, for your extensive answers and for the work of PRM on behalf of those who are suffering, these refugees and displaced persons, and look forward to seeing you again very soon. Thank you.

Sec. RICHARD. Thank you.

Mr. SMITH. I appreciate that very much, we all do.

I'd like to now welcome our second panel. The Commission is very pleased to welcome Shelly Pitterman, the UNHCR Regional Representative for the USA and the Caribbean. During his 30-year career with UNHCR, Mr. Pitterman has served on the ground in Sudan, Guinea, Burundi, as well as the UNHCR headquarters in Geneva and, of course, here in Washington. He also was seconded to the U.N. work relief of UNWRA, the U.N. Relief and Works Agency, where he worked with the Palestinian refugees in Jordan.

Thank you for joining us, Mr. Pitterman.

We'll then hear from Ambassador of the Republic of Serbia to the United States Djerdj Matković. Ambassador Matković has served as Serbia's ambassador to the U.S. since February of this year. Before his time in Washington, he was the foreign policy adviser to the Serbian Prime Minister Vučić. His country currently holds the OSCE chairmanship for 2015.

So thank you, Mr. Ambassador, for being here.

We'll then hear from Sean Callahan, chief operating officer of Catholic Relief Services, the official international humanitarian agency of the Catholic community here in the United States. Mr. Callahan is responsible for overseas operations, U.S. operations and human resources and for ensuring CRS's fidelity to the mission to preserve and uphold human life, and they have done a magnificent job.

I mentioned being in Stenkovec, Macedonia at a refugee camp. And I've lost track of the number of times I've been in a refugee camp and I saw the CRS initials on the baseball cap. Thank you so much for the work that you have done and CRS has done.

And lastly, the EU Ambassador to the United States David O'Sullivan, who is currently the senior representative of the European Union in Washington. Prior to his current appointment, Ambassador O'Sullivan served as chief operating officer of the European External Action Service, the EU's diplomatic service where he assisted the EU's high representative for foreign affairs and security policy in ensuring the consistency and coordination of the EU's external policies, strategies, instruments, missions, and the 140 EU diplomatic delegations throughout the world.

We deeply appreciate the appearance of Ambassador O'Sullivan here today as a gesture of friendship and cooperation with the European Union. We recognize that the normal congressional oversight authority over witnesses does not hold for diplomatic witnesses, and we recognize his official relationship to the United States Government.

Ambassador, O'Sullivan, thank you again for taking the time out, and all of you for being here to provide your expertise, guidance and wisdom to the Commission.

I'd like to begin now with Mr. Pitterman.

SHELLEY PITTERMAN, REGIONAL REPRESENTATIVE TO THE UNITED STATES AND CARIBBEAN, OFFICE OF THE UNITED NATIONS HIGH COMMISSIONER FOR REFUGEES (UNHCR)

Mr. PITTERMAN. Thank you very, very much, Mr. Chairman. It's, for me, a great honor and privilege to be here. It's my first time since I took up my assignment as the regional representative of UNHCR in 2013.

So much has already been said by you, Mr. Chairman, and others, by Anne Richard as well in relation to the current situation, the numbers, the reasons for flight and so on, so I will not repeat those remarks, and therefore try to keep it short.

But I did want to nevertheless mention a few numbers that have not been stated and a couple of other themes that might also provoke some conversation.

It's important, I think, to remember that now we are at more than 60 million refugees, forcibly displaced people around the world. That translates to 42,500 people every day. There have been more than 15 new conflicts in the last five years and none of the old conflicts have been resolved, so we are also witnessing the low point in the numbers of people who are voluntarily returning to their countries. And so we are facing not only protracted situations and new emergencies, we are facing protracted emergencies.

And the first and foremost on our agenda as the U.N. refugee agency is the mega crisis in Syria and Iraq, which for the first time in years has now hit Europe. As the high commissioner said, the poor have come to the home of the rich and the world has taken notice.

More than 643,000 people have arrived through Greece and Italy. The trends of the flow have changed over recent months from the Central Mediterranean to the Eastern Mediterranean and the movement that is now very much on our television screens and newspapers. Yesterday's images, I don't know if you saw them on the BBC, at the border between Serbia and Croatia, I was shocked myself and I believe it's just unbelievable that that's happening these days, people in wheelchairs stuck in the mud in freezing-rain temperatures.

That having been said, it's clear that this is overwhelmingly a refugee movement. These are people who were forcibly displaced from their homes. Ninety percent of the people who are arriving are coming from the 10 top refugee-producing countries in the world; Syria first and foremost, as well as Afghanistan, Eritrea, Iraq, Nigeria, Somalia, and Sudan.

The conflict in Syria has entered its fifth year, there's no end in sight. As we spoke earlier, you made reference, Mr. Chairman, to the lack of hope, to the desperation, to the increasing impoverishment of refugees, leading them now to take the hard decision, even in the cold as we're seeing these days, to cross to Europe.

Like all other refugee movements, stemming the tide is not an effective policy objective. Building barriers, as we've seen in some European states, or pushing back refugees, as we've seen in other European states, it doesn't end elsewhere around the world, simply doesn't work.

To quote the high commissioner for refugees, "Those who believe that the easy solution is to close doors should forget about it. When a door is closed, people will open a window. If the window is closed, people will dig a tunnel. If there's a basic need for survival, a basic need for protection, people will move. Whatever obstacles are put in their way, those obstacles will only make their journeys more dramatic."

And now we're seeing in Europe, we're seeing it as well in Central America, that there is then a temptation, a need for refugees to resort to smugglers and traffickers in order to find security and safety.

What matters is the management of the flow, not stemming the tide. And in Europe, there's evidence that the flow has not been very well managed up until now. And there is a pressure by force of circumstance, but also leadership in Europe and in the European Union to resolve that and to address the problem in a more unified and coherent way.

UNHCR is active itself in trying to find a comprehensive solution, first by focusing on saving the lives of refugees and addressing humanitarian protection needs, especially at the points of transit, first arrival, and destination.

We're working hard to, as well, strengthen protection systems through capacity building for asylum procedures in Europe, but also in the eastern Horn of Africa from where some of the refugees are coming, as well as from North Africa, and reinforcing the availability of protection and solutions in the regions where they first find security and safety.

So we have been working to provide emergency lifesaving assistance, strengthening first-line reception capacity, providing information, simple matters such as even interpretation, protection monitoring, advocacy, working with the civil society and focusing as well on unaccompanied and separated children, of whom there are several thousand who have been registered to date.

We think that the United States has a key leadership role to play, always has and hopefully always will, not only in terms of humanitarian funding, a subject which has been already discussed, where we have the gaps and where we count on Congress and the State Department to provide support, but also in terms of humanitarian diplomacy and resettlement.

Most refugees want to return home. But because of the conflict, wars and persecution, many refugees are unable to repatriate, they live in perilous circumstances, and so we identify those who require a resettlement solution for their own protection, as well as part of a strategic approach to burden-sharing.

According to the UNHCR current assessments, about 10 percent of Syrian refugees, about 400,000 people, will need resettlement over the coming years. And we focused our resettlement efforts on identifying and referring the most vulnerable refugees in Jordan, Turkey, Lebanon and Iraq, as well as in Egypt.

So far we've referred more than 45,000 Syrians for refugee resettlement globally, with 20,000 made to the United States. And as you mentioned earlier, Mr. Chairman, we're quite encouraged that there is now an acceleration of the process of processing of refugees for resettlement to the United States.

One point that hasn't been mentioned before that I'd like to highlight now is that UNHCR's been encouraging states to offer other legal avenues for access to safety and security. Resettlement is one, but we see as well family reunification, other types of humanitarian visas as an opportunity for Syrians and other refugees for that matter to gain access rather than having to risk dangerous journeys in order to arrive in a secure place. And this might also address the willingness of the diaspora community to receive their family members from countries of asylum now.

But still, resettlement will remain a solution for only a small percentage of the Syrian refugees, and that's why there has to be a comprehensive international response to the Syrian humanitarian crisis, one that also includes robust humanitarian assistance to Syrian refugees and to the governments and communities where they're hosted in Turkey, Lebanon, Jordan, and Iraq.

This will have to be accomplished with development actors and with development budgets as well. As the high commissioner said in his closing remarks to the Executive Committee earlier this month, there is no way that global humanitarian budgets will be able to face the enormous challenges related to the dramatic growth of the humanitarian problem in the world.

UNHCR, therefore, appeals to the United States to continue to exercise leadership in helping refugees in the host communities and asylum countries to recover and grow after the trauma of flight, because the U.S. Government and the American people know better than most just how richly refugees and migrants can indeed contribute to the political, economic, and cultural fabric of the nation.

Thank you very much, Mr. Chairman.

Mr. SMITH. Thank you so very much, Mr. Pitterman.

Ambassador Matković.

DJERDJ MATKOVIĆ, AMBASSADOR OF THE REPUBLIC OF SERBIA TO THE UNITED STATES

Amb. MATKOVIĆ. Thank you, Mr. Chairman. Chairman Smith, ladies and gentlemen and the members of the Helsinki Commission, thank you for the invitation to testify before you today on the issue of the migrant crisis Europe. I would like also to thank you for organizing this important hearing which highlights the fact that the complexity and the magnitude of this problem makes it incumbent upon all of us to give full and serious attention to it.

I'm here to offer the views of the Republic of Serbia, the chair country of the OSCE, as well as a country which is at the very center of the western Balkan migration routes.

Today's global migration scenario shows how migratory movements are driven often inseparably by traditional economic pull and push factors, as well as by instability and lack of security in a growing number of countries.

The migrant crisis bursting through and over political, administrative, and civilization borders speaks tellingly of the interrelatedness of far-away countries and peoples, highlighting the consequent need for a responsible and an adequate approach to the quest for a lasting and comprehensive solution to this burning issue.

Partial and limited steps are not a solution. In the process of solving this problem, the support of all the member states of the most important multilateral organizations, including the OSCE, is of paramount importance.

The OSCE region is witnessing the largest influx of refugees in decades. Apart from being a significant economic challenge, this is a process with potentially very serious security implications and, of course, of concern in regards to respect for human rights.

As the international community is struggling to find responses that reconcile refugee protection and human rights commitments with security considerations, the OSCE for its part reflects on the role it will play in supporting the shared interests of its participating states and Mediterranean partners for cooperation.

As the first, largest regional security arrangement under Chapter 8 of the United Nations Charter, the OSCE is in a distinctive position to contribute to the handling and resolution of the crisis. Its comprehensive and multidimensional approach to their security is a unique asset.

It is worth mentioning that the OSCEs do not have a mandate to tackle the crisis directly. The organization is actually dealing with the security challenges obviously derived from the migrant crisis, primarily human trafficking, transnational criminal activities and threats, as well as border management.

While the primary responsibility for these commitments lies with the participating states, the OSCE is mandated with reminding us for our commitments and assisting the participating states in implementing them.

Traditionally, OSCE decisions have largely framed its mandate on migration within the second dimension. As a result, the Office of the Coordinator for Economic Environmental Activities has been tasked with assisting the implementation of OSCE commitments, particularly in the areas of comprehensive labor, migration management, gender aspects of the labor migration policies, as well migration data collection and harmonization.

Over the years, the OSCE has also widened its third dimension mandate, including issues related to migrant integration and the protection of human rights and of the vulnerable migrant groups. The Office of Democratic Institutions and Human Rights promotes the development and the implementation of legal regulatory frameworks that respect the rights of migrants, with special attention to the most vulnerable categories.

In this context, I would like to underline that during the negotiations on the OSCE budget for 2015, Serbia, as the presiding country, has supported the proposal by the U.S.—[inaudible]—the Helsinki Commission to enhance activities in the field and fight against human trafficking to increasing the budget of the ODIHR.

OSCE field operations have also been increasingly involved in migration-related activities and projects, although they have been unevenly mandated reflecting the diversity of arrangements with host countries and different political priorities and needs.

As the presiding country, Serbia recognizes the importance of these issues and is trying to provide more active and concrete approach to the OSCE in addressing them. In light of this bleak security situation and looming instability, it is paramount that all the mechanisms that were designed and adopted by the participating states, to oversee the implementation and commitment, are strong and functioning.

This year, the Serbian parliament has promoted a set of dramatic discussions on migration and human trafficking, including in the framework of the OSCE Security Committee and the [humanitarian?] contract group.

In May, the Serbian chairmanship co-organized with the OSCE Transnational Threats Department the 2015 OSCE Annual Police Experts Meeting which focused on trafficking in human beings and illegal migrations within the context of fighting against organized crime.

At the initiative of our presidency, a joint meeting of the Security Committee, the Economic and Environmental Committee and the Human Dimensions Committee on Migration was held in Vienna on October 6.

As the OSCE chair country, Serbia supports the position of the United States by which concrete ideas for OSCE activities in terms of migration crisis should be put into the context of the preparation for the upcoming Mediterranean Conference in Jordan, as well as the OSCE Ministerial Council in Belgrade.

The Serbian chairmanship is pursuing a package of Ministerial Council decisions for the forthcoming meeting in Belgrade. As they start negotiating in the coming days, we intend to incorporate into the draft decision as many concrete recommendations as possible.

Mr. Chairman, allow me to point out that Serbia is not dealing with this crisis only in the capacity of the OSCE chair country. The migrant wave from the conflict-ridden areas has not bypassed my country. While Serbia is not the final destination for most of the migrants and refugees, it has found itself at the very center of the western Balkan migration route. And almost all migrants and refugees coming from Syria, Afghanistan, Iraq, and other unstable areas have transited through it, heading to the countries of Western and Northern Europe.

It is important to note that the numbers of migrants on the western Balkan route are constantly rising since 2009, and thus, this is not a completely new problem. What is essentially new is that in the past few months we are facing a dramatic increase in their numbers. From the beginning of this year, the Republic of Serbia has registered over 240,000 irregular migrants, with tendencies such that these numbers will only increase.

The migrants who enter our territory are being registered and provided with accommodations, food, and medical care. The way in which we dealt with this pressure and in various aspects of the migrant crisis, namely our approach and empathy that was demonstrated so far, were very positively evaluated both by EU institutions and EU member countries as well as the migrants themselves and by the Arab countries.

However, it is obvious that the burden we bear during this crisis is becoming increasingly difficult. Specifically, aside from the financial costs of the current crisis, Serbia is, for almost two decades now, dealing with over 500,000 refugees and internally displaced persons from the wars from the former Yugoslavia in the 1990s.

In a nutshell, all of the experiences we've had during this period have demonstrated that the solution for this crisis cannot be based on partial and local steps, such as closing borders or building fences. Cooperation and coordination within the international community is a must. It is necessary to reach a comprehensive and sustainable solution as soon as possible at the EU level, to include also transit countries of the western Balkan route.

We wish to be part of this common solution and we are ready to take our share of responsibility. I can assure you that Serbia will continue to be a credible EU partner and treat the migrants in a manner that is fully consistent with European and international standards.

We are also committed to actively participating in the implementation of the agreed solutions. Aside from greater solidarity, there should be an increased willingness for a political response to the root of the crisis. This means more readiness to seek a comprehensive solution and for creating conditions for sustainable peace and development in the region affected by the crisis.

The alternative is much worse. And that could lead to further worsening of the situation that would grow into a humanitarian crisis with hardly conceivable consequences.

At the end, I would like to emphasize that although a small country, Serbia is ready to cooperate with the EU, the United States, neighboring countries, and the international community in working for a peaceful and lasting solution.

Thank you for your attention and I'm looking forward to your questions.

Mr. SMITH. Ambassador Matković, thank you very much for your testimony.

I'd like to now yield the floor to Mr. Callahan.

SEAN CALLAHAN, CHIEF OPERATING OFFICER, CATHOLIC RELIEF SERVICES

Mr. CALLAHAN. Chairman Smith and esteemed members of the Committee, thank you very much for calling this hearing together, particularly as it addresses the needs and safeties and well-being of hundreds of thousands of people.

I am Sean Callahan, the chief operating officer of Catholic Relief Services which is the official overseas relief and development agency of the Catholic Church of the United States. And we serve a hundred million people annually in over a hundred countries throughout the world.

We are also a member of Caritas International which is a network of 200 different country offices throughout the world, and that is our natural partner network.

I recently traveled to the Balkans to witness firsthand the response to the refugees that CRS was doing there. And CRS is currently working with many of its Caritas partners in the most affected countries.

In a region that historically had religious strife, we found a great vibrancy in inter-religious work there and Catholic Relief Services, working closely with the Catholic community, the Orthodox community, and the Muslim community, to address the needs of the local communities as well as the migrants coming in.

In addition to that, we're working very closely with the local governments and increasing that coordination as we move forward.

I would also like to say that we're also receiving not only great generosity from people within the United States, but also Islamic relief and the Mormon Church here to have an interfaith effort as far as the resources go. And this is supporting that effort in Europe. So we're using private funding to assist these people and we've committed over 2 million [dollars] in the coming year.

I'd also like to give a nod to the ambassador as in Serbia we did notice firsthand, as I was on the border right between in Shid, right on the border of Serbia and Croatia, where thousands of people had been this weekend, and we noticed the outpouring of the Serbian people. And frankly, I think Serbia could be an example in the way that many of the people there were coming together to assist the refugees. In some countries, it seems to be pulling it apart; and in Serbia, it's actually pulling people together. So I think we should highlight that great example of Serbia and maybe see if we can duplicate that in other areas.

Who are the people that are coming and who are the people that we've seen? I think one of the examples was a young man named Khalid who came with his wife and his four children, who we saw on this no-man's-land border where many of the people rested. They rest between the border of Serbia and Croatia because they're afraid of being caught in one country or another, and so they were in the no-man's-land there.

Their home had been bombed in Aleppo and completely destroyed. They were threatened in that community and had to leave. And we asked how they got here, and Khalid said, "I was swimming alongside the boat with Ronya, wrapping her arms around me and clinging her head to my neck. It was a rubber boat and very slow so I could keep pace." Ronya is two and a half years old.

Khalid's eight-year-old daughter spoke up and told us proudly, "My daddy is very strong. When we went from Syria to Turkey, he walked over hills and mountains and most of the time he was carrying Joud and Ronya in a backpack and sometimes he carried me."

So despite the generosity and hospitality of the governments of Jordan, Lebanon and Turkey, the scale of the suffering and the need has outpaced their ability to respond to the refugee crisis, both from Syria and Iraq.

CRS and our partners have assisted nearly 800,000 people and spent over 110 million [dollars] in the last three years in response to this crisis, some addressing the crucial, immediate needs of people, but also trying to provide livelihoods to people so that they can eke out a life and so that they don't have to migrate.

Although the Holy Father has called all of us to reach out to those people who do migrate, we are working very hard to work with the local countries and communities there to ensure that people don't have to migrate, that there is security and opportunity from them in these countries in the region.

But the conflict has entered a new phase. Many have given up the idea of returning to Syria anytime soon. But unless their children can go to school and parents can provide for their families in the refugee host communities, then local integration is unrealistic.

Many of the refugees in Lebanon and Jordan, particularly religious minorities, have not registered with the U.N., and many are living outside with local communities. And as the assistance contracts, they move on to other locations.

There's been many questions on why young men—and as they're coming—and we found that if a family member can find work, they will send back remittances. The rest of the family can remain in the region where the cultural and family ties and the cost of living make life easier. Similarly, the cost of transporting a whole family, for many of these people at this time after four years of war, is too great for them to transport the whole family because many do have to pay traffickers to allow them to cross various borders.

Similarly, the issue that you raised earlier, Mr. Chairman, conscription, is a big issue. Those coming out of Syria cannot come out legally out of Syria. They have to sneak through the lines. They're either conscripted by the government or by a local rebel group, and so they sneak in and then try to get out of the local countries so that they're not sent back.

As global leaders in the international humanitarian and refugee response, the U.S. and Europe must heed Pope Francis' call and find new ways to alleviate the suffering and protect the vulnerable. We at Catholic Relief Services, and our partners with Caritas International throughout Europe, give six different recommendations.

The first recommendation, as the Holy Father has called, is let's work tirelessly and urgently to end the conflict. Stop the violence. Stop the arming of these different groups that are going there. And stop the terrible efforts of ISIS. But the governments should galvanize greater support for a regional strategy to support medium-term integration of humanitarian and development assistance to the refugee host communities. We need to help the refugees not just survive but thrive and integrate into the local communities. If we don't do that, then they will be on the move.

We need to respond to the fluid situation in Europe and we need to have BPRM be able to be a little bit more flexible to support agile international nongovernmental organizations because, as we noticed when I arrived in Belgrade, there were many people filling parks in the center city. Within the next week they were bypassing Belgrade and going right to Sid. We need to have that agility so that we could set things up. It was fortunate that the international actors that were there could, within a moment's notice, ship their people to the border. And the opportunity in Serbia was ideal as the local population was providing assistance as well.

We also would support that Congress robustly fund the humanitarian and development assistance, as it has for the last four years, at current or beyond current levels. And we do strongly support the Senate Emergency Supplemental Initiative to boost that effort, and hope that the House would agree.

We want to redouble our efforts at protection—and you brought this up, Mr. Chairman—particularly education for children. We find that it's crucially important for children to have education because it stops the abuse. You get to see the children. You get to view them at that time. And we have found many of the children require psychosocial help, and we've got innovative ways of working with puppets and others that allow the children to express the horrors they've seen. And frankly, it's allowed some of their parents to as well, because they have all suffered great violence.

And then we would also ask the administration, as Senator Shaheen has said, to expedite and increase the number of refugees settled in the United States. Eighteen to 24 months means that these people will be on the road, will not see an opportunity in the future, and they need to know their future in the short term.

Again, I thank you for hosting this hearing here, and happy to answer any questions.

Mr. SMITH. Mr. Callahan, thank you very much. And now I'm very pleased to welcome Ambassador O'Sullivan.

DAVID O'SULLIVAN, AMBASSADOR OF THE EUROPEAN UNION TO THE UNITED STATES

Amb. O'SULLIVAN. Mr. Chairman, members of the Commission, ladies and gentlemen, thank you very much indeed for taking the initiative to organize this event. And thank you for the strong commitment which members of the Congress have shown, those here present and others who have traveled to the region. And we in Europe are very grateful for the interest and attention which you give to this very difficult issue.

And, Mr. Chairman, it's already been a long afternoon. I've submitted a written statement. I suggest it be entered in the record. May I just make a few remarks so as not to take up too much time and allow for more interactive discussion?

As everyone has said, this is, first and foremost, a human tragedy. It is probably the worst humanitarian crisis in a generation. And as has been pointed out, it also is primarily a refugee crisis. This is extremely important in terms of the legal rights of the people involved.

As Assistant Secretary Richards said, we in Europe don't have the luxury, when people come knocking on the door seeking asylum, of telling them to go away and let us think about it. They have to be received immediately because we have legal and international commitments which we take very seriously, which means they must be granted immediate possibility of shelter, of care, and the possibility to make their case and have their file processed.

Now, we've been doing this for many, many years and it has all worked extremely successfully, and Europe has been a major destination for asylum seekers and refugees. What has changed, frankly, is the scale and the numbers, which have simply overwhelmed the system. And I think to the extent there are deficiencies, it is because of that.

And I would just like to remind people that I think there's been a great deal of compassion and humanity shown all across Europe. I think what the people of Italy have been doing, the people of Greece when this crisis first hit through the Mediterranean, they've opened their homes, their town halls, their schools. They've provided shelter and food. They've shown great generosity and compassion. Islands like Lesbos, which I think has a population of 80,000 people, has seen 350,000 refugees transit. It's clearly unmanageable for these countries to face this kind of crisis.

We acted immediately to try and stem the situation in the Mediterranean with the two naval forces that you've mentioned, the search and rescue operation, which has saved nearly 120,000 lives, and an anti-smuggler naval operation designed to try and break the business model of the smugglers. This has, to a certain extent, stabilized the situation in the Mediterranean, but of course it has immediately created a new flow through the Western Balkans, which has now produced the crisis that we're now dealing with. And here we have tried to firstly help the member states of the European Union who are in the front line by offering to relocate asylum seekers from the frontline states. That's 160,000 people to be located elsewhere and whose files will be treated elsewhere in the European Union.

We are offering assistance—technical assistance—to the member states to help with the processing of the applications and also to help with the very difficult issue of returning those whose asylum claims are rejected. And this is a very difficult issue because it's complicated, but our processing for asylum seekers takes, on average, about four months. But at the end of that time you do have to make some choices. People who are granted asylum have the right to stay. People who are not, we have to find out how they are dealt with, and dealt with correctly.

It's clear from all of this that the system which worked well in Europe for the last couple of years, notably the Dublin principle that the country of first arrival is the country that takes the responsibility, is no longer workable faced with this crisis. And since this crisis will probably continue, the Commission has made it clear we will need to rethink the system and will be making proposals both to have a permanent resettlement scheme but also to have a revision of our asylum procedures so that in the future we can handle these kind of situations much more nimbly and much more effectively.

Of course it is very important—and this has been said many times—that the people we're experiencing in Europe as refugees are only a small percentage of the total number of displaced people. And I want to support everything that has been said about the need to support the neighboring countries—Lebanon, Jordan and Turkey—and also other countries in the region who are experiencing difficulty, and particularly the push factor.

And I agree with everything that Assistant Secretary Richards said about the falloff of funding for the international agencies. The European Union, as member states we're the largest donor of humanitarian assistance in the world. We're the largest donor of humanitarian assistance in this region and have been for the last four years. We have stepped up our assistance, additionally. The United States is also a major donor. I think we are doing our share. I think we do need to insist that others do more in order to try and ensure that the conditions in which people are living in these countries enables them to have a decent existence and perhaps somewhat to reduce the pressure they may feel to move elsewhere.

Also we need a political solution to the sources of this conflict; Syria obviously, an end to the violence, some political process to let the people of Syria rebuild their own future. We're fortunate that at least in Libya, which was a major transit problem due to the breakdown of law and order, there has been a positive political evolution. We hope we can build on that.

So my major point, Mr. Chairman, is simply to say that this is certainly a crisis which is affecting Europe massively, but it is actually truly a global crisis, as the representative of UNHCR has said. And I think we do need a global effort. We're extremely grateful for all that the United States has done as a donor, as a political ally, but I think we all need to increase our efforts.

We would hope that the United States will continue its diplomatic engagement with us and all relevant international partners to try and find a political solution to the root causes of the refugee crisis, reaching out to third countries, encouraging them to be more receptive to refugees but also increasing the amount of money to the U.N. agencies—World Food Program, UNHCR. There is desperate under-funding. We need a major international effort.

We would be grateful if some consideration could be given to increasing the number of Syrian refugees taken in the United States. We're grateful for the numbers which have been mentioned. We would also appreciate if some—and we appreciate it's difficult and a sovereign decision of the United States, but some effort on reducing the processing time, which is indeed quite lengthy. We all need to push for increasing the funding through the U.N. system.

So, Chairman, that's really all I will say in addition to my written submission. We're very grateful for this opportunity. It's a huge challenge. We really, in Europe, are very committed to facing this challenge. I think we can be very proud of much that has been done. Perhaps some things could have been done differently or better—I would not deny that—but we will continue to face this crisis with the full basis of our humanitarian values, our commitment to treating refugees fairly and decently, and to providing, hopefully, assistance where it's needed, but most importantly political solutions which get to the root causes of why people flee their homes. Thank you.

Mr. SMITH. Thank you so much, Ambassador O'Sullivan. You mentioned increasing the number of asylum slots or refugee slots. With all due respect, what do you think it ought to be?

Amb. O'SULLIVAN. Sir, I——

Mr. SMITH. It's a tough question but I don't——

Amb. O'SULLIVAN. Any increase would be welcome. I mean, we appreciate this is a matter ultimately for the United States to decide, but clearly this problem is going to be with us for some time. We're going to have to find ways of offering these 11 million displaced people some possibilities of diverse places to build a future and we hope that the United States could play its part in that.

Mr. SMITH. Thank you.

I'll ask all of you these questions, and answer whichever ones you would like. But with winter fast approaching, obviously the threat of disease, of people dying from exposure to cold and bad weather is increased markedly, particularly with so many people in transit. And I'm wondering if there's some early warning surveillance on how we might mitigate that threat. We're always worried about a breakout of a new pandemic, and obviously that looms large, I think, in the affected region with so many people potentially going to get sick.

And maybe, Mr. Callahan, you might want to speak to what you're finding and what others are finding—and all of you might want to speak to this—in terms of diseases, the morbidity as well as the fatality rates. We know that children are less likely to be getting their immunizations. We know that other opportunistic infections will seize upon all of this transition and all of this chaos. And people do get sicker in more torn areas. And if you might want to speak to that, I would appreciate it.

I would ask you also, do Christians and those of other religious minorities face any unique challenges not faced perhaps by the Sunni or the Shia? We know that in some refugee camps some of the Christians are less likely to be housed there, that there are problems sometimes with an integration issue. So I'm wondering if they are left further behind when it comes to refugee protection and asylum seeking. Do they have unique problems?

The WFP shortfall, the World Food Program shortfall, if that were to be alleviated quickly, and other humanitarian gaps that exist, as Mr. Pitterman pointed out so well, would that likely lead to stemming the number of people who are uprooting, or has this now become a movement that is going to run its course, so to speak, as people just leave?

And again, I thought your two megatrends, coupled with the trigger, I think so well put it. You know, people don't expect this war to end anytime soon. They have spent down to the point of gross impoverishment, and now in comes the WFP cuts and the other cuts that have just made life beyond miserable. But if that were reversed, if the humanitarian crisis from that point of view were to be very robustly attacked, what would happen there?

You mentioned, Ambassador O'Sullivan, about the Dublin regulation, and we all know that means the country where they first make their presence are the ones who need to adjudicate whether or not they're asylum-eligible, but we all know that some of the countries have less capability in that area.

And I know that our own Director of Intelligence Clapper, our FBI Director Comey, the Special Presidential Envoy for the Global Coalition to Counter ISIL Allen, have all publicly expressed concerns about terrorist groups like ISIS posing as refugees, especially at those European countries where there might be a less capable effort to weed them out. And I'm wondering—you did indicate that that's being looked at. It seems to me that would be a—if you could elaborate on where that might go.

And finally—I guess that's enough for now—if you could.

Mr. PITTERMAN. Let me perhaps focus in on the question regarding what would happen if the funding pipeline was replenished in WFP and everybody was able to respond to the needs of the refugees in the countries of asylum, so in the principal countries of Lebanon, Turkey, Jordan, Iraq, to a lesser extent Egypt.

I think that the answer is that people would continue to flee from Syria. There would continue to be internal displacement. The attacks of these last days in Aleppo are said to have generated 70,000 new people moving. So it wouldn't stem the tide, once again, because their refugees, they would simply perhaps be less compelled to leave their first countries of asylum to go to Europe or elsewhere, but it wouldn't relieve the pressure on the international community to still provide support to the host countries in a bigger and better way, in a more sustained and multiyear manner rather than year to year—actually it's quarter-to-quarter humanitarian assistance.

And it would perhaps also focus more attention on the legal avenues for people to leave Lebanon and Jordan and Turkey through resettlement, through family reunification and other means, which would allow for a more managed, predictable approach to arrival in Europe as well as to the United States. That's the best-case scenario.

Mr. SMITH. And before the rest of you answer, if you could—and maybe you would want to touch on this as well—with regards to human trafficking and the exploitation of women, are there assessments being undertaken to look at the situations where women are more vulnerable? I have a whole list of places—I mentioned Munich as just one of those—where women have been raped and they've been sold into slavery. And we all know how the exploiters just have capability to find these women and sell them and reduce them to commodities.

And I know we all care about it. I know the European Union has done yeoman's work on combating these crimes. But I'm wondering if, given all of the chaos, if enough is being done and your recommendations on that.

Mr. PITTERMAN. Very good. I know for a fact that this is a matter of particular interest to UNHCR and to our partners and to the states. There's no question about that. I don't have with me specific references, but we can certainly furnish them to theCommittee when I get back to the——

Mr. SMITH. I appreciate that very much.

Amb. MATKOVIĆ. If I may answer two of your questions regarding the disease which you have mentioned and the bad weather which is coming. Of course it is a great concern in Serbia. We are trying to assist the refugees as much as possible and trying to give them accommodation, food and warm clothes, because most of them they are coming from areas there is no harsh winter conditions.

So we are trying to do that, but of course Serbia's capacities are limited so that's why we need the assistance from the European Union. And I am thankful that the EU has allocated already 1.5 million euros for these purposes, but actually we need more. We have established some refugee centers and registration centers on the border with Macedonia, with Bulgaria, and also on the leaving side towards Hungary and Croatia.

As far as these diseases are concerned they are present, and there are medical experts who can aid these refugees currently in Serbia, although I have to stress that the destination country of most of them is not Serbia. They are just in transit. The average stay in Serbia is about three to four days. So that limits, actually, the possibility that there are some diseases already happened, that people were sick and even some of them died, and also women giving birth to children, but all of these were taken care of by the medical team.

And the other question which you have mentioned regarding the treatment of the various nationalities and their religions in Serbia, all of them are treated equally. So if they are Sunnis or Shia or Christians, it is no difference. We are treating them with dignity and we are welcoming them and trying to help them, because Serbian people were also, in the past, subjected to some situations similar to this and we really understand their plight and why they are leaving their own country.

So if it would be the situation, my opinion is that we have to work together, the whole international community, with the lead of the United States, to slow the crisis at the roots, and in that way the refugees—the number of refugees will be much smaller. Thank you.

Mr. CALLAHAN. Just to pick up on those two points, winterization, it is something that we're working on right now, getting proper clothing and structures in place, because as we see—and they need to be portable structures because of the points of migration constantly changing. So we're looking at that as well as bathrooms in some of the host countries, with the porta potties and things like that.

We have had medical teams out and there is an increase in respiratory diseases, skin diseases, as you might imagine, because people haven't been able to bathe in weeks. We're talking to families that have been going for 10 weeks at a time. And so those are very difficult. I think in some of these circumstances you do have to worry about—in the longer term, if you get more and more people packed in some of these no-man's lands the issues of other diseases spreading would be more rapid.

To jump on the issue of the Christians, we haven't noticed as much in the current migration, but certainly when Christians have left both Syria and Iraq they are not going into camps because, frankly, they don't trust those communities and are integrating into local communities where they have someone that they know that they can trust in those areas. And I'd say that's both for Christians and Yazidis. They also aren't seeking the same refugee protection because they're outside of that.

And you mentioned the issue of trafficking. I think not only is there an issue of trafficking of women, but because of the vulnerability of the refugees, children are much more susceptible. The parents go out doing things. They leave children behind for someone to take care of. And we've found more and more cases of children being abused, which is just heartbreaking. And so it's one of those cases that, to get them out of these situations, we need to make sure that they have emergency schooling and that they have caregivers that provide that opportunity so their families aren't vulnerable.

Amb. O'SULLIVAN. Chairman, on your point about the Dublin agreement—and as you say, just for those not familiar with the jargon, it means, within the European Union, the first country where a person claims asylum is the country that processes the application and looks after the person while that is happening. And this used to work quite well, and I don't think there was a problem of technical ability of any country to process such asylum seekers until we got to the point of large numbers where the system has now been overwhelmed.

And also, as the ambassador of Serbia said, in many cases people don't want to stay in the first country where they've arrived. They actually want to go somewhere else. So the struggle now is simply to have some form of registration, some fingerprinting, some minimum photographing, and then allowing them to travel on.

So that's why we will certainly need to revisit this as the basic principle of asylum seeking in Europe. I don't know exactly what the Commission will come forward as an alternative, but clearly in the short term we are giving strong assistance to member states who feel overwhelmed with the numbers they have to deal with to help them cope better with the numbers and process the claims better.

On the security issue—I mean, you discussed this at some length with Assistant Secretary Richards—I don't want to say that there is no risk, but to be very frank, the calculation on the European security level—and this is not a European competence; it's a national competence, but they generally feel that this is not a high risk at the moment. Frankly, the terrorist acts we've had in Europe have often come from homegrown terrorists. And there are other easier ways for people to get into Europe if they want to as terrorists than disguising themselves as refugees and having to accept to be fingerprinted and photographed. And I'm not so sure that this has to be our major concern.

I'm not saying that we do not need to be aware of it. I'm not saying that—the security forces, I'm quite sure, are keeping a close eye on the people who are claiming asylum and whose files are now with them with fingerprints and photographs. And I'm not saying that we may not develop problems in the future, particularly if we are unable to integrate these people who are granted asylum and who may become alienated in our societies. Then I think we could face some challenges. But I think in the immediate term this doesn't have to be our major concern, and I think we need to allay public fears rather than fuel them.

And I agree entirely with Mr. Callahan about the young men. I think those of us of Irish origin remember well that it was often easier for an income earner to be the first person to move and to leave the family behind and then to send money back or eventually to seek family unification when you'd actually built up a livelihood. And it's a fairly tough journey from those countries to anywhere in Europe, and I'm not surprised that it's the young, fit men who feel more able to make it than people with families, or that man who was carrying his children on his shoulder. So I think those are just some elements I would put into the discussion.

Mr. SMITH. Just if I could follow up, if you don't mind. There have been reports that funding for Macedonia, which is obviously an area that's been very much impacted by the inflow, is inadequate. Is that something the European Union is looking at to beef that up because so many people have come in through Macedonia?

Amb. O'SULLIVAN. Well, I mean, what we are firstly trying to deal with the influx coming onto the European territory, European Union territory, for which we're legally responsible. But we are working very closely with all the neighboring countries because we understand that, as the UNHCR representative said, I mean, nobody thinks that you can build a wall and stop this, but it is a question of how you can manage it and how you can avoid trying to fix it in one place. You simply spill the problem over into a neighboring country and then into another neighboring country.

That's why we really need an integrated effort across the region with good cooperation between us, and also financial burden-sharing to help everyone contribute to helping this to be done in the most humane and correct way vis-à-vis the refugees, and hopefully, in due course, to slow down the flow and persuade people that maybe they don't have to rush to get inside the European borders; there is a better future which may be elsewhere for them.

Mr. SMITH. Commissioner Shaheen?

Ms. SHAHEEN. Well, thank you very much. And thank you to all of you both for being here this afternoon and for the work that you're doing to address this crisis.

I want to first agree with the statements that have been said. What I saw when I was in Europe was a tremendous outpouring of native people in Greece, in Germany—I heard of that and other places where people were trying to respond to the humanitarian effort. And while they were overwhelmed, they were trying to do the right thing, and I think people deserve a lot of credit for that. I'm sure in Serbia that's also the case.

And I think certainly leadership from countries like Germany to say that this is a crisis that we should all respond to is important to recognize. And we met with the coast guard in Greece who, often at great personal risk, had rescued literally thousands of people from the Mediterranean who were saved because of that heroism.

I also agree with everything that's been said about the need to support Lebanon, Turkey and Jordan, because they have certainly taken in so many refugees. And, Mr. Callahan, thank you for putting a face on these refugees. We talked to some young men in a settlement house in Berlin who were students who had fled, wanted to continue their education and wanted to go back to Syria because they wanted to be the future leaders of that country.

I have three just questions before we close this afternoon. And the first has to do, Ambassador, with—one of the things that surprised me in Germany was hearing how many of the refugees who had come there were from the Balkans, mostly from Albania and Kosovo. And, appreciating the history in the Balkans, you may want to hand that question off to somebody else, but can you talk about why you think we're seeing those large numbers of refugees from the Balkans? Most of this discussion today has focused on Africa and the Middle East, but, in fact, we are seeing those refugees. And what is the response to those folks who have left those Balkan countries?

Amb. MATKOVIĆ. Thank you, Senator, for this question. And yes, you are right that a big number of refugees have left, recently, the Balkans, mainly from Kosovo, Albania, but also some from some other countries. And the reason I think is more economic, that the economic hardships, the lack of jobs, the level of unemployment and a lack of perspective for their future lives. So they think that they will find a better life in Western Europe and that it will be their future.

But in order to solve this problem I think we have to work together, and all these countries in the region should be united on an agenda to promote the economic relations with all the Western European countries and the United States and to attract more investment, to create conditions for more foreign investment. Once they have a better life there and they have possibilities for jobs and a livelihood there, they will stay.

So the root problem in the Balkans is economic reasons, much like in Syria or in other countries. But yes, I can compare it with some African countries who are also leaving for economic reasons. My prime minister, Mr. Vučić—and thank you very much receiving him last time he was here—has really a very good agenda on the regional reconciliation in the countries. That's why his first visit as prime minister was to Bosnia Herzegovina to show our support to the united and one country Bosnia Herzegovina. And also he visited, as you know, Albania twice, and the Albanian prime minister, Mr. Edi Rama, was in Belgrade.

So this regional reconciliation and the problems which we are doing is, I think, the whole—the solution of the whole problem.

Ms. SHAHEEN. And I certainly applaud that leadership and very much appreciate it.

One of the things that we heard was—we know that many of the African migrants are coming across through Libya, as has been talked about, many coming from Turkey across the Mediterranean to Greece. One of the things that we heard was that there are traffickers operating out of Turkey and that there is the potential to help crack down on those traffickers in a way that would help with the problem. To what extent do you all see the international community or the EU working with Turkey to try and address those traffickers who are contributing to immigration, Mr. Pitterman or Ambassador O'Sullivan?

Amb. O'SULLIVAN. I think the consensus is I should answer that question, Senator. [Laughter.]

I mentioned the naval mission that we put in place, and I was—I don't know if there's a legal difference between people—smugglers and traffickers, but basically both types of activity are at work here. And it is clear that in the early stages of this crisis this was particularly true in Libya, people paying large sums of money to come a very convoluted route and then being put in unseaworthy vessels, pushed out to sea and then phone calls to the Italian coast guard to say a boat's going to sink if you don't rescue it—extremely cynical and dangerous.

And we have put in place a stable mission which basically will operate across the whole Mediterranean with a mandate. We've not got a—we're very grateful to the United States for the support for that—a U.N. mandate to operate on the high seas. We would hope that we could reach an agreement with a new Libyan administration also to help them address this issue on their shores. And we're engaged in conversations with Turkey, as you know, actively now to see how we can jointly work with them to try and deal with this issue of illegal movement into Greece, which you've been able to witness it firsthand.

So yes, I mean, I think we're actively engaged. We have a naval force that's out there trying to make some inroads. It's not easy, but I think we need to deal with the smugglers. Of course it will not—once again, this is dealing with a symptom, but we need to deal with it—the bigger problem will still remain but this is one aspect I think we definitely need to address.

Ms. SHAHEEN. Yes, one of the things that we heard is that as migrants were put into the big rubber boats—and that's exactly what they are, big rubber rafts—that they were told when they get close to the shore to cut them so they will begin to sink so that the coast guard would come and rescue them.

As you point out, this is—whether it's the smugglers or whether it's humanitarian efforts, it's a response to the immediate challenge. The longer-term challenge is how do we address the conflicts that are causing—or the economic conditions that are causing the refugees? But also, what about the reintegration efforts, because one of the things that we heard was that that's a longer-term challenge. It's probably a more-expensive-in-the-long-term challenge, and it's one in which often members of EU countries are more concerned about addressing. And certainly the United States has seen that here in terms of the immigration challenges that we have in the United States.

So can you speak to, Ambassador O'Sullivan, the discussions at the EU and what you are looking at that will address that longer-term reintegration challenge, and how that is being looked at across EU member states?

Amb. O'SULLIVAN. Well, we have a long history of migration within Europe. Almost every European country has significant populations either from within Europe in previous generations or from North Africa or Turkey—3 million Turks living in Germany, very substantial North African populations living in France and Belgium. Even in more recent times my own country, Ireland, has now got 250,000 Poles living there, and some 60,000 Chinese, I believe.

So the world has changed, and I think we are conscious that in some cases the integration of these communities has been more successful than others. And I think people are very conscious that looking forward—and we can now assume, I think, that we are going to have a fairly consistent flow of refugees and asylum seekers, and possibly even economic migrants that we're going to have to face and deal with. I mean, we'd like to deal with the root causes. We'd like to feel that people didn't have to come. But on the other hand, we also have a demographic situation which maybe would mean that we actually might have economic needs for migrants.

And I think people are very conscious of trying to think through now, how do we ensure the integration; how do we ensure language training, access to education? President Juncker, the president of the Commission, made a very strong appeal that all of these asylum seekers should be allowed work, which is not necessarily the case for people with pending applications for asylum, because he said not only the dignity of work but the integration and the sense of belonging to a community.

So I think, yes, there's a lot of thought going into it. We're dealing with the immediate crisis, but the next phase is definitely—well, given that these people are now here and probably will continue to come, perhaps in slightly smaller numbers, but it doesn't matter. We really need in each member state to have a conscious policy of how we make sure that they are successfully integrated into our respective societies, yes.

Ms. SHAHEEN. So we will stay tuned for——

Amb. O'SULLIVAN. Yes, well——

Ms. SHAHEEN. ——further decisions at the EU level?

Amb. O'SULLIVAN. Unfortunately it's not something that you see the results of two days afterwards.

Ms. SHAHEEN. Sure.

Amb. O'SULLIVAN. I think we need to stay tuned and come back in five years' time to see how successful we've been.

Ms. SHAHEEN. Well, thank you all very much. Thank you——

Mr. SMITH. Thank you.

48

Ms. SHAHEEN. ——Chairman Smith, for holding the hearing.

Mr. SMITH. Thank you very much, Commissioner.

Mr. PITTERMAN. If I may just add a quick word on this point, because UNHCR has been quite proactive, I think, together with other resettlement countries, to help promote dialogue, to provide a convening for that. And the U.S. has quite a lot to learn from the resettlement experience in Europe, but up until now that experience has been very much the social welfare state model, dealing with tens, hundreds of people. Now, au contraire, they're confronted with quite important numbers of refugees being resettled or relocated within Europe, much like the American model.

And so, as Assistant Secretary Richards said, they're also asking questions, and the United States can provide, I think, some very helpful answers, with the imperative to work. But the United States hasn't really set up standards for citizenship. We don't know how many refugees who have been resettled have become citizens of the United States, and the other data indicators aren't always very clearly available.

But the main thing now that's happening, I see, is a lot more engagement by, for example, the Migration Policy Institute, where they're having experts in integration of refugees and immigrants in Europe speaking to Americans to learn more about how things are—how things are happening and where there are lessons to be learned. But it will be a long-term thing.

A lot of what we've been talking about today—if I may just, as a sort of summary, closure remark from my side—first, the refugees are, like you said, a symptom of the problem. They are victims. They're not choosing to go. They're not—while they may be of economic importance, that's not their primary motivation, after all.

But what we're in for now is the long term, whether it's—and it's big bucks, frankly, in terms of reconstruction in Syria when there is a solution—and Iraq—in terms of development assistance to the host countries in the interim, and also to encourage other middle-income asylum countries like Tunisia and Kenya and Ethiopia and Cameroon to continue to provide asylum to literally hundreds of thousands of refugees, very much at their expense, because there is no way that UNHCR is able to support host communities at the same level as we provide support to refugees, and that there will be, therefore, a continuing need for development aid. And it's a big challenge ahead of us, and I think it's—we're talking Marshall Plan.

Mr. SMITH. Thank you. Anyone else like to—concluding?

Thank you so much for your expertise, your extraordinary commitment to humanity, which is played out every single day. You have provided this commission with a tremendous number of insights and recommendations that we will work on as individual members of the Senate and the House, but also as a commission. So thank you so very much. The hearing is adjourned.

[Whereupon, at 4:39 p.m., the hearing was adjourned.]

APPENDIX

PREPARED STATEMENTS

PREPARED STATEMENT OF HON. CHRISTOPHER H. SMITH, CHAIRMAN, COMMISSION ON SECURITY AND COOPERATION IN EUROPE

Good afternoon and welcome to everyone joining us this afternoon as we inquire into the European refugee crisis and how the US, EU, and OSCE should respond.

The Syrian displacement crisis that has consumed seven countries in the Middle East has become the biggest refugee crisis in Europe since World War II. At least 250,000 people have been killed in Syria's civil war, many of them civilians.

The security forces of Syrian dictator Bashar al-Assad's security forces have been responsible for many of these killings, targeting neighborhoods with barrel bombs and shooting civilians point-blank. ISIS has committed genocide, mass atrocities, and war crimes, against Christians and other minorities, and likewise targeted, brutalized and killed Shia and Sunni Muslims who reject its ideology and brutality.

Fleeing for safety, more than four million Syrians are refugees, the largest refugee population in the world, and another 7.6 million Syrians are displaced inside their home country.

Syria's neighbors, Jordan, Lebanon, Turkey, Iraq, and Egypt, are hosting most of these refugees. Before the Syria crisis, these countries struggled with high rates of unemployment, strained public services, and a range of other domestic challenges. Since the conflict began, Syrians refugees have become a quarter of Lebanon's population, and Iraq, which has been beset by ISIS and sectarian conflict, is hosting almost 250,000 refugees from Syria.

Until this past summer, few Syrian refugees went beyond countries that border their homeland. Syrian refugees and migrants from a range of countries have since come to Europe in such large numbers, and so quickly, that many European countries, especially front-line entry points like Greece, transit countries like Serbia, and destination countries like Germany, have been challenged to respond.

The UN High Commission for Refugees, UNHCR, reports that more than 635,000 refugees and migrants have arrived in Europe by sea in 2015. Fifty three percent of these people are from Syria, sixteen percent from Afghanistan, six percent from Eritrea, and five percent from Iraq. Notably, only fourteen percent of them are women, twenty percent are children, and the remaining sixty five percent are men. The European crisis requires a response that is European, national, and international, and the United States is essential to it. There must be effective coordination and communication directly between countries as well as through and with entities like the OSCE and European Union. Individual countries also must have the flexibility to respond best to the particular circumstances in their own countries.

The response must address "push" factors, like economic challenges and aid shortfalls in countries like Syria's neighbors that have been hosting refugees. It must also address "pull" factors, like decisions individual European countries have made that have attracted refugees.

There is real human need and desperation. Refugees are entrusting themselves to smugglers and where there is human smuggling there is a higher risk of human trafficking. I am especially concerned about the risk of abuse, exploitation, and enslavement, of women and children. Already we are hearing reports that some European countries are failing to protect women and girls from sexual assault and forced prostitution. The lack of separate bathroom facilities for males and females, rooms that can be locked, and other basic measures, enable such attacks. There is no excuse for such failures and everything must be done to ensure that women and children are safe.

There is also the real threat that terrorist groups like ISIS will infiltrate these massive movements of people to kill civilians in Europe and beyond. I am deeply concerned that the screening at many European borders is inadequate and putting lives at risk. All of us must be responsive to the humanitarian needs without compromising one iota on security. European response plans should include specifics about strengthening security screening throughout the European region.

During the conflict in Kosovo, I travelled to Stenkovec refugee camp in Macedonia and was at the McGuire Air Force Base in New Jersey to welcome some of the 4,400 people brought from there to the United States. A refugee—Agron Abdullahu—was apprehended and sent to jail in 2008 for supplying guns and ammunition to the "Fort Dix 5"—a group of terrorists who were also sent to prison for plotting to kill American soldiers at the Fort Dix military installation.

Given Secretary Kerry's announcement in September that the United States intends to resettle at least 85,000 refugees in fiscal year 2016, including at least 10,000 Syrians, and at least 100,000 refugees in fiscal year 2017, the United States and Europe must be on high alert to weed out terrorists from real refugees. Because religious and ethnic minorities often have additional risks and vulnerabilities even as refugees, they should be prioritized for resettlement.

This hearing will examine the "who" is arriving, the "why" they are coming to Europe, and the "what" has been done and should be done in response. European governments, entities like the OSCE and the EU, and civil society all have critical roles to play.

The United States has been the leading donor to the humanitarian crisis inside Syria and refugee crisis in the region. We also have the largest refugee admissions program in the world. However, according to the testimony of Shelly Pitterman, Regional Representative for the UN High Commission for Refugees, who we will hear from soon, "The current inter-agency Syrian Regional Refugee and Resilience (3RP) plan for 2015 is only 41% funded, which has meant cuts in food aid for thousands of refugees." Globally, he warns, "The humanitarian system is financially broke. We are no longer able to meet even the absolute minimum requirements of core protection and lifesaving assistance to preserve the human dignity of the people we care for. The current funding level for the 33 UN appeals to provide humanitarian assistance to 82 million people around the world is only 42%. UNHCR expects to receive just 47% of the funding we need this year."

This hearing will look at how the United States can best work with our allies in Europe to meet humanitarian needs and prevent security threats.

In the 20th and 21st centuries, the United States and Europe have come together to address the great challenges of our time and this is an opportunity to do so again.

PREPARED STATEMENT OF HON. BENJAMIN L. CARDIN, COMMISSIONER, COMMISSION
ON SECURITY AND COOPERATION IN EUROPE

Ladies and gentlemen, I join my colleagues in welcoming our witnesses to this hearing before the Helsinki Commission today.

The current crisis facing many of our fellow OSCE participating States is both unprecedented and heartbreaking. Not since World War II has Europe seen such a massive movement of people across the continent. According to estimates, more than 600,000 people have entered Europe so far in 2015. That's nearly the entire population of Baltimore.

According to UNHCR, an organization we'll hear from shortly, most of those currently entering Europe are fleeing war or persecution, in Syria or elsewhere, and more than meet the criteria of the 1951 Geneva Refugee Convention. Many of these refugees have suffered tremendously.

No parent should ever have to be put in the desperate position of Alan Kurdi's father, weighing the potential danger of flight against nearly certain death at home. Sadly, we know the end to that tragic story.

The United States and other countries must continue to address the underlying causes that have propelled so many people to leave their homes in search of a better life. But while we seek to address the security and economic challenges that are part of the current crisis, we must not lose sight of human rights and humanitarian aspects of the crisis.

Government conversations thus far have primarily focused on hardening European borders, discouraging refugee travel from transit countries into the Schengen zone, and the security threat of refugees. Noting that the original comprehensive definition of security contained in the Helsinki Final Act rested on the pillars of human rights and fundamental freedoms, it is incumbent upon the long-term stability of the transatlantic relationship that humanitarian and sustainable strategies increasingly become part of the conversation.

To that end, I share concerns that government officials from countries whose own refugees were given shelter in 1956, 1968, and 1981 have shown far less empathy for the displaced and uprooted today. Hungary's decision to militarize its border, as called for by the extremist Jobbik party, and its use of tear gas and water cannons on migrants, including children, is contrary to humanitarian norms.

Ignoring the potentially destabilizing effect that an influx of refugees may have over time on fragile and blossoming governments in neighboring non-EU countries like Serbia, Macedonia, and Turkey, and OSCE Mediterranean Partners, like Jordan, is only a precursor for other possible issues down the road.

Serious conversations on long-term resettlement plans for refugee populations throughout Europe must accompany efforts that currently seek to house large numbers of refugees in border states.

With experts estimating many refugees will not be able to return to their homes for a decade or more, the need for long-term sustainable planning for integrating refugee populations to complement processing and sheltering efforts is critical. Employment, education, delivery of services, participation in public life, and mechanisms to address discrimination are only some of the concerns integral to national resettlement plans.

Building comprehensive and inclusive plans that guard against the creation of two-tiered systems that prioritize new arrivals over existing refugees and migrants is another.

Addressing the exorbitant increase in anti-migrant rhetoric from political leaders and others is vital to advancing wide-ranging humane resettlement efforts, and if unaddressed can fuel anti-migrant violence. For instance, the German government has reported nearly three times as many attacks on homes for asylum seekers this year compared to last year linked to fearmongering.

I commend Chancellor Merkel for standing up for the dignity of asylum seekers and addressing the long-term benefits of integration initiatives.

In my role as OSCE Parliamentary Assembly Special Representative on Anti-Semitism, Racism, and Intolerance, I am not only charged to monitor these situations, but also facilitate solutions. As such, I have introduced legislative provisions in the Senate calling for joint action between our nations to address discrimination and foster inclusive societies.

Again, thank you to each of our witnesses for making the time to appear before us today. I look forward to your testimony.

PREPARED STATEMENT OF SHELLY PITTERMAN, REGIONAL REPRESENTATIVE OF THE
UNITED NATIONS HIGH COMMISSIONER FOR REFUGEES (UNHCR)

Introduction

Mr. Chairman and members of the Commission on Security and Cooperation in
Europe, on behalf of the Office of the United Nations High Commissioner for Refugees (UNHCR) I would like to express our appreciation for the opportunity to appear before you today to address the refugee crisis in Europe.

My name is Shelly Pitterman, and I am the Regional Representative for the
United States and the Caribbean in Washington, D.C., a position that I have held
since 2013. During my tenure I have repeatedly seen the critical role of the Helsinki
Commission in shedding light on numerous humanitarian crises. Our office has enjoyed an excellent working relationship with the Commission, and we look forward
to continued collaboration.

Overview of UNHCR

UNHCR is the UN refugee agency mandated by the international community to
ensure refugee protection and to identify durable solutions to refugee situations
around the globe. With a staff of nearly 9,500, of which about 88% are located in
deep field and hardship locations, we work tirelessly to assist the world's most vulnerable people. UNHCR's mandate and international law define a refugee as a person who has a well-founded fear of persecution based on reasons of race, religion,
nationality, membership in a particular social group, or political opinion. While refugees remain our core constituency, our populations of concern also include internally
displaced persons (IDPs), asylum seekers, and stateless persons. In certain situations, we have also helped provide protection and assistance to victims of natural
disasters.

The vast number of the forcibly displaced and the growing complexity of the
causes of displacement make our work and the work of our partners both more challenging and more needed than ever before. We recognize and greatly appreciate this
Commission's ongoing support of UNHCR and your concern for vulnerable people
worldwide.

Global displacement at historic heights

Today's global displacement situation is unprecedented. There are currently more
than 60 million refugees, asylum seekers and internally displaced persons worldwide as a result of conflict and persecution. Last year, only 126,000 refugees were
able to return to their homes, the lowest number since 1983. Fifteen new conflicts
have broken out or reignited in the past five years, while none of the old conflicts
were resolved. The number of people forced to flee their homes each day due to conflict or persecution stood at 42,500 last year. That's a small city fleeing each day.
The interlinked mega-crises in Syria and Iraq, which have uprooted over 15 million
people, are powerful examples of this evolution—but not the only ones. In the last
twelve months alone, 500,000 people have fled from their homes in South Sudan
and 190,000 from Burundi. Some 1.1 million were newly displaced in and from
Yemen, and 300,000 in Libya. In the Asia-Pacific region, 94,000 people have crossed
the Bay of Bengal and the Andaman Sea since 2014 in search of protection and a
more dignified life. Tens of thousands, many of them children, are fleeing horrific
gang violence and abuse in Central America. And there has been little or no im-
provement in the crises affecting the Central African Republic, Nigeria, Ukraine,
the Democratic Republic of Congo, and elsewhere.

As these crises grow, so does the politicization of refugee resettlement and aid.
A major challenge to the safety and protection of refugees arises from toxic public
debates and the climate of fear they engender. In some countries around the world,
there has been a proliferation of xenophobic narratives and inflammatory statements—both at the political and civil society levels. This contributes to a hostile en-
vironment, which has in some instances even led to violent attacks against refugees.
In this climate, we need an all-out effort to ensure that protection—and in particular, the institution of asylum—remains life-saving, non-political, and fundamen-
tally humanitarian. Today's problems desperately require a depoliticized space in
which we can get on with practicalities, such as shelter, necessities of life, and the
determination of who is in need of refugee protection.

The European Crisis

As of October 13, more than 590,000 people have arrived in Europe through
Greece and Italy so far this year. September alone saw 168,000 arrivals (mostly in
Greece), five times the number from the year before. In total more than 3,000 people
have tragically died or gone missing during their journey. The stories and photographs of families packed into flimsy boats fleeing for their lives, camping in train

stations and in the open air with just the clothes on their back, and fleeing from sometimes brutal police and border agents, have shocked the world. The conflicts in Syria and Iraq have spilled beyond that region, and the effects can now be felt throughout much of Europe as the humanitarian community struggles to provide enough assistance. Make no mistake, Europe is facing its biggest refugee influx in decades.

UNHCR is calling upon the European Union to provide an immediate and life-saving response to the thousands of refugees as they are crossing the Mediterranean and making their way through Europe. We are also calling upon the European Union to relocate thousands of refugees throughout Europe. We currently predict that that up to 700,000 people will be seeking safety and international protection in Europe by the end of 2015. While it is difficult to estimate at this point, it is possible that there could be even greater numbers of arrivals in 2016.

Who is coming and why?

Despite the extreme risks and difficulties of the trip, UNHCR continues to see thousands of people arriving in Europe every week. Although most attention is focused on Syrians, it should be noted that they are not the only refugee population making this journey. While Syrians comprise 70% of the sea arrivals to Greece, the top ten refugee producing countries represent over 90% of such arrivals. The other main nationalities of refugees and migrants arriving in Greece are Afghans, Iraqis, Nigerians, Pakistanis, Somalis, and Sudanese. All of these countries have been marked by conflict, violence and persecution. Without peaceful solutions to these crises, people lose hope and seek other options for themselves and their families. Many are resorting to smugglers to bring them to a safer haven and are clinging to the hope that a life in Europe can provide a better future for their children, one with peace and education. Of the total arrivals in Europe, 18% are children.

Syria crisis

While the refugee crisis in Europe is due to protracted conflicts in a number of different countries, the ongoing deadly conflict in Syria has become the main source of refugees. As the conflict in Syria has entered its fifth year with no end in sight, more than 4 million Syrian refugees have fled to neighboring countries. Continued danger inside Syria and deteriorating conditions in the host countries are now driving thousands of Syrians to risk everything on perilous journeys to Europe. The spike of Syrian refugees coming to Europe this year is mainly due to three factors—two long-term trends, and a more recent trigger.

First, many have lost hope that a political solution will soon be found to end the war. Second, after so many years in exile, their resources have run out and living conditions have been steadily deteriorating. Seven out of ten Syrian refugees in Lebanon live in extreme poverty, and in Jordan 86% of refugees in urban areas live below the Jordanian poverty line. The vast majority of Syrian refugees in Jordan live in urban areas rather than in camps, which is also the case in the other host countries. Refugees across the region are unable to work legally, and over half of their children are not getting any education. This situation of poverty among urban Syrian refugees is a major concern.

The third factor—the trigger that has encouraged many refugees to make the journey to Europe—is the humanitarian funding shortfall. UNHCR has been struggling to continue supporting the growing number of extremely vulnerable families with cash and shelter items, especially ahead of the coming winter. A few months ago, a lack of funding forced the World Food Program to cut their assistance by 30%. As a consequence, many refugees felt that the international community could be starting to abandon them.

To break down the causes for flight even further, UNHCR staff have identified the following seven core factors behind this movement based on observations and conversations with refugees in Jordan, Lebanon, Egypt and Iraq.

Loss of hope

Hope is dwindling for many refugees. Feelings of uncertainty about the future are compounded by miserable conditions, are fueling a sense of despair and desperation.

High costs of living/Deepening poverty

Refugees in Lebanon cite the high cost of living as a factor in deciding whether to stay or go. In Egypt, refugees say it is getting harder to pay rent, manage high levels of indebtedness and provide for their basic needs. In Jordan, the inability to provide for one's family was the most common reason cited by people who knew someone who had left.

The cumulative effect of four years in exile with restricted access to legal employment was also said to be taking its toll. In many cases savings are long depleted, precious valuables have been sold off, and many refugees across the region live in miserable conditions, struggling to pay rent, feed their families, and cover their basic needs.

Limited livelihood opportunities

Without the ability to work legally, many refugees struggle to make a living. Lack of livelihood opportunities or access to the formal labor market was cited as a problem by refugees in Lebanon, Egypt and Jordan. Syrian refugees in Iraq say the large number of internally displaced Iraqis has increased competition for jobs in the Kurdistan region of the country. Meanwhile, work on construction sites in the region has dried up with the drop in oil prices.

The lack of access to legal work leads refugees, desperate to provide for themselves, to resort to informal employment—risking exploitation, working in unsafe conditions or having payment withheld by unscrupulous employers. If caught working illegally, some refugees face sanctions, for example in Jordan being returned to a camp. Under new regulations in Lebanon, refugees must sign a pledge not to work when renewing their residency status.

Aid shortfalls

Aid programs for refugees and host communities in the region have been plagued by chronic funding shortages. The current inter-agency Syrian Regional Refugee and Resilience (3RP) plan for 2015 is only 41% funded, which has meant cuts in food aid for thousands of refugees. Those refugees still receiving food aid must survive on about 50 cents a day. Many refugees in Jordan told UNHCR that the WFP food aid cuts were the last straw in their decision to leave the country. Tens of thousands miss out on cash assistance, sinking deeper into debt. As a result, people resort to negative coping strategies—including begging, child labor, and increased indebtedness. Shrinking humanitarian aid was cited by refugees in Iraq, Jordan, Lebanon and Egypt as cause of desperation and a driver of onward movement.

In Jordan, inadequate funding has caused refugees to lose free access to healthcare. As a result, almost 60 percent of adults with chronic medical conditions do without medicine or health services, up from 23 per cent in 2014. There is also a marked decrease in access to curative and preventative health care.

Hurdles to renew legal residency

In Lebanon, new regulations for Syrian refugees have made it harder for Syrians to reside in the country legally. Increasingly, therefore, Syrians transit through Lebanon to Turkey. Refugees already in Lebanon must pay US$200 per year to renew their stay. The Syrians are required to sign a pledge not to work and must present a certified lease agreement. Many refugees are fearful of arrest or detention and feel vulnerable because of lapsed residency visas.

In Jordan, an urban verification exercise was launched by the authorities in February to ensure that all Syrians residing outside of camps are issued with a new identity document in order to access services. This exercise has presented a number of challenges, including the cost of obtaining a health certificate (JD30/US$42 for those over 12 years of age) as part of the process.

Scant education opportunities

Limited education opportunities were cited as a problem for refugees in Jordan, Egypt, Lebanon and Iraq. Education is highly valued among Syrians, who enjoyed free and mandatory schooling at home before the war. The worsening conditions that refugees face in exile are having a devastating impact on the education of refugees. In Jordan, some 20 per cent of children are abandoning school in order to work, and in some cases girls are being forced into early marriage. Some 90,000 Syrians of school age have no formal education, with 30,000 of those accessing informal education and the rest missing out completely.

In Lebanon, where education is free to Syrians in a two-shift system, many children struggle to attend while at the same time working to support their families. While the Ministry of Education has doubled the number of places for Syrian children (that is, 200,000 in the 2015/2016 school year), another 200,000 Syrian children will be out of school this year. Across the region, Syrian youth are missing out on tertiary education and losing hope for their future.

Feeling unsafe in Iraq

In addition to the large numbers of Syrians leaving the neighboring countries for Europe, Iraqis are also undertaking the journey. Violence by armed militias has created deep insecurity in Iraq, with recent months noting increased improvised explosive devises (IEDs) and suicide attacks in Baghdad. According to the most recent International Organization for Migration (IOM) displacement update, 3.2 million people have been displaced in Iraq since January 2014. The majority of displaced Iraqis UNHCR spoke to who were travelling outside Iraq reported feeling unsafe in their country. In particular, many Iraqis from minority groups told UNHCR that they see migration as the key to their physical safety. These reasons have driven thousands of refugees to look beyond neighboring countries and undertake the dangerous journey to Europe to find shelter.

Response in the EU

Over half a million refugees and migrants have arrived on Europe's shores since January of this year. Even on a continent of more than 500 million inhabitants, five thousand people arriving daily is a very significant number. But it is not an unmanageable one—provided that things are properly handled. The decision taken by the European Union to internally relocate 160,000 asylum seekers is a key step in the right direction, but much more is needed for this system to work well. The solution will include the creation of adequate reception centers near the entry points, with sufficient capacity to receive, assist, register and screen tens of thousands of people, together with more legal migration avenues for those in search of protection. Immediate efforts must be undertaken to ensure adequate reception facilities and to provide humanitarian relief items in the European countries where refugees first arrive, such as Greece and Italy, and in the countries refugees travel through on their journey north. While there have been improvements in reception conditions in the last few weeks, there is an immediate need for more reception capacity and infrastructure, sanitation facilities, and core relief items such as warm clothing as the weather worsens.

Implementation of the European Union's relocation program is critical. The EU Ministers for Justice and Home Affairs met on September 22 in Brussels and adopted a decision on the relocation of an additional 120,000 people in need of international protection from Greece and Italy. UNHCR welcomes the news of the departure of the first relocation of refugees in the EU. Recently, 19 Eritrean asylum seekers were relocated from Italy to Sweden, as the first step in a process that envisions the relocation of 150,000 people from Italy and Greece to participating EU states.

UNHCR strongly urges EU member states to unite behind the emergency proposals negotiated on September 22, to manage the refugee and migration crisis that is becoming increasingly chaotic and unpredictable. As the High Commissioner for Refugees stated, "The relocation plan will not put an end to the problem, but it will hopefully be the beginning of a solution." UNHCR additionally urges a substantial and rapid increase in legal opportunities for refugees to access the EU, including enhanced resettlement and humanitarian admission, family reunification, and humanitarian and student visas. Without such avenues, refugees will continue to be left with few options, and the increase in international efforts to crack down on smugglers and traffickers is unlikely to be effective.

UNHCR reiterates its deep conviction that only a united European emergency response can address the present refugee and migration crisis. Europe can no longer afford to continue with this fragmented approach that undermines efforts to rebuild responsibility, solidarity and trust among States, and is creating chaos and desperation among thousands of refugee women, men and children. After the many gestures by governments and citizens across Europe to welcome refugees, the focus now needs to be on a robust, joint European response.

UNHCR's Response

UNHCR is promoting a three-pronged comprehensive response to the European refugee crisis: a) saving lives and addressing humanitarian and protection needs at points of transit, first arrival and destination; b) strengthening protection systems through capacity building for various asylum procedures in the East and Horn of Africa, North Africa and Europe; and c) reinforcing the availability of protection and solutions in regions where refugees first find safety. In Europe, UNHCR's actions will support first-line reception interventions through: provision of emergency and life-saving assistance; strengthening of first-line reception capacity; provision of information; protection monitoring and follow-up; advocacy; and the provision of appropriate technical assistance and other support to national and local authorities, as well as civil society, particularly relating to emergency reception arrangements. UNHCR is also working with local partners to ensure adequate identification and response for women, men, boys and girls at particular risk, such as unaccompanied and separated children. This includes working to ensure prevention and response to sexual and gender based violence, access to child protection systems, and services for those with specific needs.

Specifically, in close cooperation with relevant government counterparts; EU institutions and agencies; international partners; INGOs; NGOs; local communities and civil society, UNHCR will:

- Support the creation of adequate reception arrangements and management;
- Enhance protection monitoring through direct or indirect establishment of UNHCR presence at entry, transit and exit points along transit routes;
- Provide interpretation support to local authorities and NGOs in the different countries that engage with arrivals and refugees on the move to ensure better communication, profiling and identification of protection concerns, and facilitate the swift access of persons of concern to the asylum procedure;
- Assist the authorities and other relevant institutions with the identification and registration of new arrivals;
- Enhance the provision of relevant information and counseling to new arrivals and persons on the move on: their rights and obligations upon entry of the country of transit/asylum; the risks of irregular onward movement; and means of accessing the asylum procedure, family reunification, the EU relocation program, and options for resettlement outside the EU, when applicable;
- Strengthen public information and advocacy strategies to elicit wider understanding by the public, governments and stakeholders towards refugees;
- Enhance communication efforts to reach communities in countries of origin and first asylum through a more concerted use of mass communication channels and platforms, to inform of the dangers of irregular crossings and existing and emerging legal ways to enter Europe, as well as provide accurate information on their rights and obligations once in Europe and the overall situation, with a view to manage expectations and counter inaccurate information relayed by smugglers and traffickers.

Global UNHCR recommendations

UNHCR has two main global recommendations to address this crisis.

1. Financial and Political Support

The humanitarian system is *financially broke.* We are no longer able to meet even the absolute minimum requirements of core protection and lifesaving assistance to preserve the human dignity of the people we care for. The current funding level for the 33 UN appeals to provide humanitarian assistance to 82 million people around the world is only 42%. UNHCR expects to receive just 47% of the funding we need this year. We have managed to avoid meaningful reductions of our direct support to refugee families, but at a high cost to our other activities.

In light of this, UNHCR is appealing for more funding to meet the immediate needs of the hundreds of thousands of refugees we are currently serving in Europe. Our most recent appeal highlights the need for $128 million in total financial requirements for the Special Mediterranean Initiative from June 2015 to December 2016.[1] In the current volatile and fast-changing environment, we are appealing to donors to provide contributions that can be allocated as flexible as possibly across the Europe region.

2. Resettlement

Most refugees want to return home as soon as conditions allow; unfortunately continued conflict, wars and persecution prevent many refugees from being able to repatriate. Many also live in perilous situations or have specific needs that cannot be addressed in the country where they have sought protection. In such circumstances, UNHCR helps resettle refugees to a third country.

Resettlement is the transfer of refugees from an asylum country to another State that has agreed to admit them and ultimately grant them permanent settlement. Resettlement is unique in that it is the only durable solution that involves the relocation of refugees from an asylum country to a third country. Of the 14.4 million refugees of concern to UNHCR around the world, less than one percent are submitted for resettlement.

According to UNHCR's current assessments, about 10% of Syrian refugees—some 400,000 persons in total—are in need of resettlement. UNHCR is focussing its resettlement efforts on identifying and referring the most vulnerable refugees in the host countries of Jordan, Turkey, Lebanon, and Iraq. These particularly vulnerable refugees include survivors of torture and severe violence, women-headed households, refugees with serious medical needs, and others who remain at heightened risk. Resettlement remains an important tool for refugee protection, while also being an impor-

---

[1] file:///C:/Users/fisherc/Downloads/UNHCRSMISBAppealJune2015–December2016–30SEPT15.pdf

tant expression of solidarity by the international community with the countries in the region that are hosting millions of Syrian refugees.

UNHCR has already referred more than 45,000 Syrians for refugee resettlement, with more than 20,000 of those referrals made to the US. Although Syrian arrivals to the US have been fewer than 2,000 persons so far, we are encouraged by the stated intent of the US administration to admit at least 10,000 Syrian refugees in US fiscal year 2016.

Resettlement of 400,000 Syrians, a number not seen since the 1980s when millions of Southeast Asian refugees were resettled, will take a concerted international commitment over the next several years. To date, more than 30 countries have pledged 130,000 resettlement and humanitarian admission places for Syrian refugees. UNHCR is calling upon the international community to expand upon this generous initial response. Towards this end, UNHCR has also encouraged states to be flexible in their immigration laws and procedures and to offer family reunion and other migration opportunities for Syrian refugees. While UNHCR recognizes the need for all states to have thorough security screening measures applied to all refugees and immigrants, including Syrians, UNHCR has called upon states to find ways to make these necessary procedures as fair, efficient and as timely as possible. UNHCR is dedicated to working with states to ensure that resettlement program remain safe and secure for both refugees and for receiving states.

I'd like to emphasize that, as is the case with other refugee populations globally, permanent resettlement to another country is—and will remain—a solution for only a small percentage of the Syrian refugees. Even if countries significantly increase the number of resettlement places and related opportunities that they offer, the vast majority of the Syrian refugees will remain in the Syria region. For that reason, resettlement must be approached as a critical part of a comprehensive international response to the Syrian humanitarian crisis; a response that also includes robust humanitarian assistance to the Syrian refugees and to the governments and communities in Turkey, Lebanon, Jordan, and elsewhere that are so generously hosting these refugees.

Conclusion

We must call upon our shared humanity, histories, and sacred traditions of providing refuge to persons fleeing conflict and persecution, and remember that it was exactly for times like these that the international refugee protection regime was created. Let us recognize the reality of human displacement, remain true to the rule of law, and acknowledge the positive contributions that refugees and migrants make to our societies. To quote the High Commissioner for Refugees, António Guterres, "This is the starting point: there is no easy solution. And so, those who believe that the easy solution is to close doors should forget about it. When a door is closed, people will open a window. If the window is closed, people will dig a tunnel. If there is a basic need of survival, a basic need of protection, people will move, whatever obstacles are put in their way—those obstacles will only make their journeys more dramatic."

Mr. Shelly Pitterman is the UNHCR Regional Representative for the USA and the Caribbean. He joined UNHCR in 1984 and served in Yei, Sudan (1984–1988); Headquarters Geneva on the Somalia Desk (1988–1990); N'zerekore, Guinea (1990–1992); and as the UNHCR Representative in Burundi (1992–1995).

During his four year tenure as the Chief of UNHCR's Resettlement Section, the Annual Tripartite Consultations on Resettlement began and the UNHCR Handbook on Resettlement was first introduced. He then established UNHCR's Regional Support Center in Nairobi, Kenya before returning to Geneva as Deputy Director of the Human Resource Management Division.

In 2005, he was seconded to UNRWA (UN Relief and Works Agency) to be the Director of Operations serving Palestinian refugees in Jordan. He returned to UNHCR in 2008 to lead UNHCR's Human Resources Management Division, a position he held until his appointment to Washington.

Mr. Pitterman is a native of New York City. He is a graduate of Brandeis University and earned his doctorate from Northwestern University.

PREPARED STATEMENT OF DJERDJ MATKOVIĆ, AMBASSADOR OF THE REPUBLIC OF SERBIA TO THE UNITED STATES

Chairman Smith, Co-Chairman Wicker, Commissioners, Ladies and Gentlemen;

Thank you for the invitation to testify before you today on the issue of the migrant crises in Europe. I would also like to thank you for organizing this important hearing, which highlights the fact that the complexity and the magnitude of this problem makes it incumbent upon all of us to give full and serious attention to it.

I am here to offer the views of the Republic of Serbia, the chair-country of the OSCE as well as the country which is at the very center of the Western Balkan migration routes.

Today's global migration scenario shows how migratory movements are driven, often inseparably, by traditional economic pull and push factors, as well as by instability and the lack of security in a growing number of local contexts. The migrant crisis, bursting through and over the political, administrative and civilization borders, speaks tellingly of the inter-relatedness of faraway countries and peoples, highlighting the consequent need for a responsible and energetic approach to the quest for a lasting and comprehensive solution to this burning issue. Partial and limited local steps are not a solution. In the process of solving these problems, the support of all of us, the Member States of the most important multilateral organizations, including the OSCE, is of paramount importance.

The OSCE region is witnessing the largest refugee influx in decades. Apart from being a significant economic challenge, this is a process with potentially very serious security implications and the cause of concern in regards to the respect for human rights.

As the international community is struggling to find responses that reconcile refugee protection and human rights commitments with security considerations, the OSCE for its part reflects on the role it could play in supporting the shared interests of its participating States and Mediterranean Partners for Co-operation. As the world's largest regional security arrangement under Chapter VIII of the UN Charter, the OSCE is in a distinctive position to contribute to the handling and resolution of the current crises. Its comprehensive and multi-dimensional approach to security is a unique asset.

Traditionally, OSCE decisions have largely framed the OSCE mandate on migration within the second dimension. As a result, the Office of the Coordinator for Economic and Environmental Activities (OCEEA) has been tasked with assisting in the implementation of OSCE commitments, particularly in the areas of comprehensive labor migration management, gender aspects of labor migration policies, and migration data collection and harmonization.

Over the years, the OSCE has also widened its third dimension's mandate, including issues related to migrants' integration and the protection of human rights of vulnerable migrant groups. The Office of Democratic Institutions and Human Rights (ODIHR) promotes the development and implementation of legal and regulatory frameworks that respect the rights of migrants, with special attention to the vulnerable categories.

Further roles and responsibilities have been progressively allocated to Executive Structures and specialized units in response to the evolving nature of the migration phenomenon, which has been shaped by the many trends that have come to characterize the increasingly inter-connected OSCE region. In particular: Conflict Prevention Center for the protection of persons at risk of displacement or already affected by it in all phases of the conflict cycle, including cooperation with specialized agencies such as UNHCR. Gender Section for addressing the specific aspirations and vulnerabilities of migrant women. Office of the Special Representative and Coordinator for Combating Trafficking in Human Beings for the protection of the rights of victims of trafficking who have been involved in vulnerable migration processes, particularly if irregular migrants. TNTD/Strategic Police Matters Unit, Border Security and Management Unit (BSMU) and Action against Terrorism Unit (ATU) for migration-related crimes, in particular human trafficking and migration smuggling as well as enhancing Travel Document Security (TDS) as an integral part of strengthening border management.

OSCE Field Operations have also been increasingly involved in migration-related activities and projects although they have been unevenly mandated, reflecting the diversity of agreements with the host countries and the different local priorities and needs.

As the presiding country Serbia recognizes the importance of this issue and is trying to provide more active and concrete approach of the OSCE in addressing it. In light of this bleak security situation and looming instability, it is paramount that all the mechanisms that were designed and adopted by the participating States to oversee the implementation of commitments are strong and functioning.

At the initiative of our presidency a Joint Meeting of the Security Committee, the Economic and Environmental Committee and the Human Dimension Committee on Migration was held in Vienna on October 6th.

In the conclusions of the meeting, among others, the following specific courses of action and proposals of activities are listed:

First Dimension: Maximum use of all three platforms (border management, the police and the fight against terrorism) for exchange of information with a special focus on the fight against trafficking and smuggling. This in particular since it has been determined that a large percentage of migrants are among the total number of victims of trafficking.

Second Dimension: Intensification of cooperation with other international organizations dealing with migratory movements, as well as activities to implement obligations in the field of labor migration.

Third Dimension: Ensuring full respect for the obligations in the field of human rights, tolerance and non-discrimination, freedom of movement, integration of migrants and so forth. ODIHR stands ready to carry out missions in the field and provide support to member countries at their request, in assessing the situation in the light of respect for human rights of migrants, asylum seekers and refugees, and respect for their freedom of movement.

As the OSCE chair-country Serbia supports the position of the US by which the concrete ideas for OSCE activities in terms of migration crises should be put into the context of the preparation of the upcoming Mediterranean Conference in Jordan, as well as the OSCE Ministerial Council in Belgrade. The Serbian Chairmanship is pursuing an ambitious package of Ministerial Council Decisions in view of the forthcoming Belgrade Meeting. Only in the field of the human dimension 9 Ministerial Council Decisions are now under consultation with participating States. As we start negotiating in the coming days, we intend to incorporate into the draft decisions as many concrete recommendations as possible.

Mr. Chairman,

Allow me to point out that Serbia is not dealing with this issue only in the capacity of the OSCE chair country. The migrant wave from the conflict-ridden areas, flooding many European countries, has not by-passed my country. Although Serbia is not the final destination for most of the migrants and refugees, it has found itself at the very center of the Western Balkans migration routes and almost all migrants and refugees coming from Syria, Afghanistan, Iraq and other unstable areas, primarily from the Middle East, have transited through it, heading to the countries of Western and Northern Europe via the two EU Member States—Greece and Bulgaria.

It is important to notice that the numbers of migrants on the "Western Balkan route" were constantly rising since 2009 and thus, this is not an entirely new problem. What is essentially new is that in 2015 we are facing a dramatic increase in their numbers. Using the figures—from the beginning of this year until the October 8th, the Republic of Serbia has registered over 200.000 irregular migrants. The tendency is such that these numbers will not subside, but only increase.

Migrants who enter our territory are being registered (including fingerprints taken) and provided with accommodation, food and medical care. The way in which we have dealt with this pressure and the various aspects of the migrant crisis, namely our approach and empathy that was demonstrated so far, were very positively evaluated by both EU institutions and EU member states, as well as by the migrants themselves and by the Arab countries.

While this can make us proud, it is obvious that the burden we bear during this crisis is becoming increasingly difficult. Specifically, aside from the financial coasts of the current crisis, Serbia is almost for two decades now, dealing with over 500,000 refugees and Internally Displaced Persons from wars in Yugoslavia from 1990's.

In a nutshell, all of the experiences we had, either directly or indirectly, during the crisis have demonstrated to all of us that the solution (or solutions) for this crisis cannot be based on partial or local steps (such as closing borders or building fences). Cooperation and coordination within the international community a must.

It is necessary to reach a comprehensive and sustainable solution, as soon as possible, at the EU level, to include also transit countries on the Western Balkan route. We wish to be part of this common solution and we are ready to take our share of responsibility, once the European Union agrees a migrant crisis settlement strategy. I would like to point out that Serbia will continue to be a credible EU partner and treat the migrants in a manner that is fully consistent with European and international standards. We are also committed to actively participating in the implementation of all agreed upon today, including comprehensive border management.

On a more global scale, aside from greater solidarity, there should be an increased readiness for the political response to the source of the current crisis. That means more readiness to seek political solutions and for creating conditions for sustainable peace and development at the source of the crisis. The alternative to such actions is much worse and that would lead to further deterioration of the situation and degenerate into a humanitarian crisis, with hardly conceivable magnitude and consequences.

Thank you for your attention.

Mr. Djerdj Matkovic was born in Subotica, Serbia, on May 28, 1955. He graduated from the University of Belgrade, Faculty of Law in 1978, International Law and International Organizations.

Career

Since February 2015: Ambassador Extraordinary and Plenipotentiary of the Republic of Serbia in the United States

April 2014–February 2015: Foreign Policy Advisor to the Prime Minister of the Republic of Serbia Mr. Aleksandar Vucic

August 2012–April 2014: Foreign Policy Advisor to the First Deputy Prime Minister of the Republic of Serbia Mr. Aleksandar Vucic

February 2012–July 2012: Chief of Protocol of the Ministry of Foreign Affairs of the Republic of Serbia

2011–2012: Director of the Department for North and South America at the Ministry of Foreign Affairs of the Republic of Serbia

2007–2011: First Counselor at the Embassy of the Republic of Serbia in Washington, D.C., USA

2006–2007: Deputy Secretary General of the Ministry of Foreign Affairs of the Republic of Serbia

2005–2006: Deputy Chief of Cabinet of the Minister of Foreign Affairs of Serbia and Montenegro

2001–2005: Minister Counselor and Deputy Chief of Mission at the Embassy of the FR of Yugoslavia (later Serbia and Montenegro) in Budapest, Hungary

1998–2001: Counselor—Chief of Cabinet of the Assistant Secretary for Bilateral Relations at the Ministry of Foreign Affairs

1993–1998: First Secretary at the Embassy of the FR of Yugoslavia in Harare, Zimbabwe

1990–1993: First Secretary—Chief of Cabinet of the Under Secretary at the Ministry of Foreign Affairs 1986-1990 Third Secretary at the Embassy of the SFR of Yugoslavia in Ottawa, Canada

1982–1986: Attaché and Third Secretary at the Department for Neighboring Countries at the Federal Secretariat of Foreign Affairs

1981–1982: Trainee at the Federal Secretariat of Foreign Affairs of the SFR of Yugoslavia

Mr. Matkovic speaks English and Hungarian; Married, spouse Vera and son Djerdj Jr.

PREPARED STATEMENT OF SEAN CALLAHAN, CHIEF OPERATING OFFICER, CATHOLIC
RELIEF SERVICES

Chairman Smith, Co-Chairman Wicker, thank you very much for calling this hearing to consider how the US and Europe can better respond to the plight of hundreds of thousands of people fleeing to Europe in recent months. Chairman Smith, your long-standing commitment to protecting the poor and marginalized across the globe and in places long forgotten is a profound demonstration of the compassion and solidarity Pope Francis asks us all to engender.

I am Sean Callahan, Chief Operating Officer of Catholic Relief Services (CRS). CRS is the official humanitarian relief and development agency of the Catholic Church in the United States. We serve nearly 100 million people annually with local partners in more than 100 countries.

I recently traveled to the Balkans to witness firsthand CRS' response to the refugees entering by the thousands every day. It is heart-breaking to imagine walking in their shoes; to imagine one's own life in such chaos. First, suffering violence in one's home community; then biding time in a neighboring country, humbly accepting charity. And then finally to conclude that your family has no future and so someone must undertake a supreme act of love and sacrifice, risking a treacherous and unknown journey so that the rest of the family may live.

Khaled, who came to Serbia with his wife and four children after their apartment in Aleppo was bombed, told us, "I was swimming alongside the boat, with Ronya (age two and one-half) wrapping her arms around me and clinging her head to my neck. It was a rubber boat and very slow. So I could keep pace."

Khaled's eight-year-old daughter, Omama, told us proudly, "My Daddy is very strong. When we went from Syria to Turkey, we walked over hills and mountains. And most of the time he was carrying Joud (six months old) and Ronya in a big backpack. And sometimes he was also carrying me."

Despite immense generosity and hospitality on the part of the governments of Jordan, Lebanon and Turkey, the scale of suffering has outpaced their ability to respond. It has also overwhelmed the capacity of the international humanitarian and refugee systems. CRS and our partners have assisted nearly 800,000 people and spent over $110 million in the last three years in response to the Syrian crisis. Many other international non-governmental organizations (iNGOs) and intergovernmental organizations (IGOs), as well as new donors like the Gulf States, have committed significant resources to respond to this crisis. Despite these generous responses, the exodus to Europe cries out that so much more must be done. As global leaders in international humanitarian and refugee response, the US and Europe must find new and creative ways to help to alleviate this suffering and protect the vulnerable. Pope Francis has led in this effort to do more by asking every Catholic parish in Europe to reach out and assist the refugees; He reminds us of our moral obligation to help the stranger.

In my testimony, I offer first, CRS' analysis of the current exodus to Europe; second, CRS' response to those in need and third, our recommendations for how to move forward not only to address the extraordinary humanitarian needs in Europe but also the longer-term needs in refugee host countries.

Exodus to Europe

During my recent visit to Europe, I was amazed by the rapid pace and fluidity with which the refugees are moving. The scale of movement is also noteworthy: as many as 6,000 people passed into Serbia one day; the average is 4,500 people a day. Most are guided by their cell phones; information from family or friends who preceded them; and social media.

The UN reports that two-thirds of the refugees fleeing to Europe are from refugee-producing countries: predominantly Syrians; while most of the others are Iraqis—largely Kurds—and Afghans. This matches CRS' experience. The Syrians are from Kobani, Tartous, and Hassake, among other places, but many had already fled Syria and had been residing in neighboring countries. Some are coming in family groups. These refugees brought only what they could carry. As the *Washington Post* and others have reported, we have come across a smattering of other opportunistic economic migrants, but they are not the majority by far. Many of the Afghans had been living in Turkey for years. Nevertheless, those fleeing are not the poorest of the poor: it costs about $3,000 per person currently to cross the Mediterranean. People are traveling using their smartphones, without guides or other assistance. They hire drivers or ride buses from one border to the next. Some report exploitation in the form of extortion and robbery. As entrepreneurial individuals offer services such as transportation, the risk of this exploitation will continue.

Most of the refugees with whom I met traveled through Greece and Macedonia; some through Bulgaria. Most did not travel by boat but rather through Turkey. Many refugees have discovered they can traverse southern Europe more quickly by bypassing the major cities such Belgrade, and the registration process. Individuals are moving astonishingly fast—spending a few hours in Macedonia. The route is very fluid, changing based on what successful travelers report out about border openings. Our partnership with faith-based organizations enables us to respond quickly to these shifts. Like way stations on a marathon route, we aim to be punctual and flexible. This response will become more challenging with the onset of winter: the need for shelter, medical assistance, and warmer clothes will increase the risk of the journey.

CRS' Response

CRS is working with partners in Serbia, Greece, Macedonia, Albania and Croatia to meet the needs of tens of thousands of refugees. As the Chairman knows, CRS operates as part of the international umbrella of Caritas Internationalis—the Catholic social service agencies throughout the world. Caritas agencies throughout Europe have been responding to the plight of Syrians, and CRS is helping them to rapidly scale up in response to the immense needs. Given the scale of need, CRS is partnering with other faith-based organizations as well. In a symbol of the healing salve of time, we are working with Muslim and Orthodox partners.

Likewise, our funding is interfaith: the Church of Latter Day Saints and Islamic Relief have funded CRS. As always, CRS is leveraging private money with public money to maximize efficiency and effectiveness. We anticipate spending at least $2 million into next year on the response in Europe, including with a grant to Caritas Germany.

Program activities include meeting basic needs. Food and emergency living supplies are being provided to families including women, children and the elderly; they include sleeping bags and mats, hygiene packages, food rations, clean water and other support. Most refugees in transit are sleeping in public parks, forests and abandoned factories. CRS and our partners in Serbia have established several large structures equipped with beds, toilets and showers to provide basic shelter and sanitary needs for the most vulnerable refugees, particularly those who returned from Hungarian border. Doctors on staff in Serbia treat hundreds of refugees at a refugee aid center near the Hungarian border. Finally, CRS and our Church partners provide critical information, legal resources, translation and language services, so refugees know their rights and can make informed decisions. As winter approaches, assistance will become more complex and more costly.

As faith-based organizations, we serve not only refugees' physical needs, but also are sensitive to their spiritual ones. For example, on September 24, we joined other aid organizations to organize an Eid celebration for Muslim refugees.

CRS and our partners' assistance throughout the Middle East runs the gamut: from distribution of non-food items and food to legal support; from medical assistance to water and sanitation. We have focused in particular on emergency education, child-friendly spaces, and psycho-social support. In one particularly innovative project, we partnered with No Strings International (the creators of the Muppets) to create culturally appropriate videos to help children process trauma and facilitate peacebuilding. Through trainings of trainers, we have exported this program throughout the region. We primarily work outside of camps, where most of the refugees live.

Why this new movement now?

A steadily growing sense of hopelessness as their situation deteriorates seems to be the catalyst for most fleeing. They can no longer live with such uncertainty for their future or their families'. Life in Syria has become too difficult and violent, but dreams cannot be realized in a country where one is but a guest.

To name violence as the cause of this flight is necessary but not sufficient. Violence is not new. Yet as it becomes more complex, the dangers weigh more heavily. A certain randomness as to who is bombing whom exacerbates the fear and uncertainty. The refugees with whom we spoke do feel that Assad is more vulnerable now. (Though it is noteworthy that this was before the Russian airstrikes began.) The unknown of who might fill that power vacuum—and the possibility that it could be a radical group—can be terrifying. Fear of the self-proclaimed called Islamic State and how it will operate overshadows communities in their proximity. Particularly in Iraq, people would not be nearly so fatalistic were it not for the presence of the self-proclaimed Islamic State.

Beginning last year, refugees with whom we work in the region began to voice despair. Many had given up the idea of returning to Syria anytime soon. And unless children can go to school and parents can provide for their families in the refugee host communities, integration into these host communities will be unrealistic. [1] We know that many refugees in Jordan and Lebanon, particularly religious minorities, have not registered with the UN and may be moving as assistance in the region contracts. Some male refugees decline to register to avoid being recruited, and some flee Syria for fear of forced recruitment.

We also know that many of the Syrians fleeing are educated and entrepreneurial. CRS and our partners have hired many: as teachers, engineers, and outreach workers. The inability to work in refugee host communities affects not only their economic but also their psychological well-being. The inability to work legally leads to negative coping strategies, including early marriages, prostitution, and child labor, among others. CRS commends the Government of Jordan for its recent authorization for refugees to work. When refugees can legally work, NGOs can engage in livelihoods programs to help them become more self-sufficient.

The remote likelihood of returning to Syria in the near future, and the possibility of finding opportunity in Europe appear to be the main reasons so many have determined that the journey is worth the risk. Some families' coping strategy, as resources wear thin, is to send one worker to Europe who can send remittances back to the family. This would enable the rest of the family to remain in the region, where cultural and family ties, not to mention cost of living, make life easier. Nonetheless, unless education and work opportunities for Syrians in Syria's neighboring countries can be vastly scaled up, the family member in Europe will almost certainly eventually send for the rest of the family.

The exodus of Syrians and Iraqis from the region signals a new phase in the Syrian conflict. Despite efforts by INGOs like CRS, local civil societies, governments, and non-traditional donors, the despair of so many refugees indicates that assistance must move beyond short-term band-aids to longer-term solutions. To that end, CRS offers the following recommendations.

Recommendations

Resolve to end the conflict. The Administration should commit to high-level negotiations towards a political solution to the conflict in Syria. As the violence escalates, the time is ripe. The Administration should work urgently and tirelessly with other governments to obtain a ceasefire, initiate serious negotiations, provide impartial humanitarian assistance, and encourage efforts to build an inclusive society in Syria that protects the rights of all its citizens, including Christians and other minorities.

To respond adequately to the situation in Europe, the Department of State's bureau of Population, Refugees and Migration (PRM) should fund international private organizations directly. The agility and speed required to respond to the scale and fluidity of this flight to Europe demands the shortest funding routes possible. By mandate, PRM gives the majority of its funding through four agencies, including UNHCR and the International Organization for Migration. Yet direct funding of operational agencies will help to get assistance on the ground faster and navigate potential governmental barriers. Staffing limitations to manage funding within PRM can be creatively solved through mechanisms such as consortia, which have worked well elsewhere.

The US government should galvanize greater support for the regional strategy—with traditional and new donors such as the Gulf States—to support medium-term integration of humanitarian and development assistance in refugee host communities. This will help families to envision a future in countries of potential integration, and reduce tension among host communities. If many refugees will remain in Lebanon, Jordan, and Turkey for the foreseeable future, a focus on helping them to thrive and integrate, rather than merely survive, should be the aim of humanitarian and development strategies. The World Bank and other development organizations do not operate in these countries because they are considered middle income; but extraordinary times in fragile states call for extraordinary measures. Development organizations can help to facilitate such a strategy by supporting the host country schools, medical facilities, and economic development, among other institutions and activities. Gulf States could help by significantly increasing their reception of "guest workers." (Those governments are not signatories to the international refugee convention, but have allowed refugees to work there.)

---

[1] There are traditionally three options for refugees in the long-term (known as "durable solutions"): return to their home country; integration in the host country to which they fled and have been living; or resettlement to a third country. Resettlement is usually a reality for less than 1% of the population.

Congress should robustly fund both humanitarian and development assistance in host countries beyond previous fiscal years. With $4.5 billion in funding to date to the region, the US has led traditional donors in assistance. We must continue robust funding and seek to collaborate with other donors, including the Gulf States, to maximize efficiency and effectiveness. Gregory Maniatis of the Migration Policy Institute estimates that an adequate response would cost on the order of $20 billion in the region and around $30 billion per year in Europe. For Fiscal Year 2016, the US should fund no less than was appropriated in Fiscal Year 2015. CRS and the US Conference of Catholic Bishops support the Middle East Refugee Emergency Supplemental Appropriations Act of 2016 (S. 2145) released last week by Senators Graham and Leahy, which, if enacted, would provide an additional $1 billion for BPRM.

Redouble efforts at protection, particularly education of children. UNICEF's No Lost Generation campaign reminds us that a child without an education will suffer throughout life. According to UNICEF, as many as 1.5 million of the refugees are children, and many of them are out of school. The cumulative impact on Syria's development will be significant. As Pope Paul VI once said, "war is development in reverse." The United States should increase its funding for emergency education and other protection efforts, including psycho-social support and child-friendly spaces.

Continue the United States' historic leadership in refugee resettlement: the Administration should significantly increase the numbers of refugees resettled in the United States. When the US helps to resettle particularly vulnerable populations, including religious and ethnic minorities and those with complex medical needs, it helps to ease the burden of neighboring countries hosting particularly large refugee populations. Our colleagues at the United States Conference of Catholic Bishops resettle a significant number of refugees in the United States and can speak to the requirements necessary to scale up. The Administration must work diligently to make resettlement more effective and efficient for these vulnerable populations.

With the UN, the Administration must strengthen support for and adherence to UN Security Council resolutions 2139 and 2165 calling for greater humanitarian access within Syria.[2] A paltry percentage of the more than 400,000 Syrians in besieged areas receive assistance, due to lack of access. Unless the United States and other actors reinforce these resolutions, both these lives and the future of international humanitarian law are at great risk.

As the chief operating officer for Catholic Relief Services, Sean Callahan is responsible for Overseas Operations, U.S. Operations and Human Resources, and for ensuring CRS' fidelity to its mission to cherish, preserve and uphold the sacredness and dignity of all human life, foster charity and justice, and embody Catholic social and moral teaching. His role is to enhance performance, stimulate innovation and position CRS for the future.

Sean's commitment to CRS
Sean was executive vice president for Overseas Operations from June 2004 to September 2012. He provided oversight for a program and management portfolio which grew to more than $700 million, serving people in more than 100 countries and engaging a team of more than 5,000 staff.

As regional director for South Asia from January 1998 to May 2004, Sean strengthened CRS' programming and partnerships in India, Pakistan, Afghanistan, Sri Lanka, Bangladesh and Nepal. He worked closely with Blessed Teresa and the Missionaries of Charity in Calcutta, represented CRS at the Asian Bishops Synod in 1998, and led the regional response to floods, droughts, earthquakes, cyclones and man-made emergencies. He experienced a terrorist attack by the Tamil Tigers at the Sri Lankan airport, and championed programming in Afghanistan during and after the Taliban's rule.

Immediately before his assignment to South Asia, he served as director of Human Resources for CRS at our world headquarters in Baltimore, and previously as the director of the CRS Nicaragua program. He also worked in other Central American locations and at headquarters in various capacities.

---

[2] Resolution 2139 (February 2014) demands that parties "promptly allow rapid, safe and unhindered humanitarian access," and Resolution 2165 (July 2014) authorizes UN humanitarian agencies and their implementing partners to provide cross-border assistance with notification to (rather than the consent of) the Syrian government.

Education and other roles

Sean holds a master's in law and diplomacy from Tufts University, where he also received a bachelor's, magna cum laude, in Spanish.

Sean is on the Board of Trustees for Catholic Charities USA (2014–present) and on the Executive Committee and Representative Council of Caritas Internationalis (2011–2015). He is also the president of Caritas North America (2015–2019).

More about Sean

Sean and his wife, Piyali, have two children, Sahana and Ryan. Sean is a member of the Church of the Resurrection in Ellicott City, Maryland.

PREPARED STATEMENT OF DAVID O'SULLIVAN, AMBASSADOR OF THE EUROPEAN
UNION TO THE UNITED STATES

I would like to thank you, in particular, Chairman Smith and your Co-Chairman
Senator Wicker, as well as the other members of the Commission for giving me the
opportunity to present the main components of the EU's response to the refugee crisis. I am David O'Sullivan the European Union ambassador to the United States,
a position I have held for just about a year and it is an honor to speak to you today
about what the press refers to as "the migration crisis in Europe."

The ongoing refugee crisis is not a European crisis. It is a global crisis, fuelled
by conflicts, inequality and poverty, the consequences of which unfolded in Europe
but the roots of which are far away from our continent. This does not mean that
we as Europeans do not have a responsibility to respond to it.

Nevertheless, we are seeking a global response to achieve a lasting solution to the
conflicts, instability and poverty, which are the main causes of the refugee crisis,
working closely with our international partners.

This crisis is also a sensitive issue for Europeans. While some of our Member
States are facing major economic difficulties, many of our fellow citizens wonder
about our capacity to welcome and integrate new waves of migrants.

However, I also want to emphasize that European citizens have offered unprecedented support to the refugees. Civil society is showing a vibrancy that often goes
unreported but is strong, moving and comforting and provides first help to thousands of refugees across Europe.

Among the many examples I have in mind, I would like to point out the incredible
signs of support expressed by Greek citizens to migrants. While Greece is still facing
a severe economic crisis, local people in islands like Kos or Lesbos have continued
to donate food and other basic supplies to help the refugees.

In Italy, a country which has encountered economic difficulties for some time, 300
families from Lombardy have responded to the appeal of the Archbishop of Milano,
Cardinal Scola, by offering to host refugees in their homes.

I also want to mention the throngs of people joining marches and vigils across Europe in a show of solidarity with refugees, with almost 30,000 people in Stockholm.
And of course, it is impossible to forget the images of Syrian migrants being welcomed at train stations in Germany and Austria.

Overview of the situation

Whether one looks at the numbers or at the images, the current refugee crisis is
of unprecedented magnitude.

We are confronted with a multi-faceted phenomenon, comprising economic migration on one side and asylum seekers on the other side, with despair and quest for
security and a better life as their common denominator. By October 2015, 710,000
migrants and refugees had entered the European Union this year, while only
282,000 migrants crossed EU borders for the whole of 2014.

I want to underline that the migration crisis is of a mixed nature, comprising economic migration on one side and "forced migration" of asylum seekers on the other
side.

It is important to keep the question of economic migrants separate from the issue
of refugees.

This calls for different types of responses from the European Union. We have a
responsibility to show solidarity and put in place the adequate mechanisms of reception for refugees. By virtue of international law, refugees have a right to protection.
No state, regardless of whether it has signed the U.N. Refugee Convention, can return a refugee to a place where his life would be endangered.

On the other hand, migrants, whose motivations are primarily economic and who
are not entitled to international protection and cannot be legally admitted will be
provided temporary accommodation, while appropriate mechanisms are put in place
for their return to their countries of origin in accordance with the international
rules and standards.

The EU response

We all understand that ultimately, only political solutions to the conflicts com-
bined with economic development in the host countries will provide a lasting solution to the migration and refugee crisis in Europe.

At the political level, we need to work hard to find solutions to conflicts such as
the ones in Syria and Libya. To do this, we need to intensify our diplomatic engagement with all relevant international partners. In parallel, a lot of work needs to be
done on the root causes of migration in the main countries of origin.

At the operational level, we continue to work hard in order to provide support to those who need it, respecting human rights and providing protection notably for the most vulnerable.

We have taken steps to deal with migration crisis a long time before it hit the headlines. We have mobilized our instruments, with three objectives: (i) to save lives, (ii) to ensure protection to those in need and (iii) to manage borders and mobility.

- We launched rescuing operations Poseidon and Triton and tripled our presence at sea. Over 122,000 lives have been saved;
- Member States have agreed to relocate 160,000 refugees from Greece, Italy and other Member States directly affected by the refugee crisis. On October 9th, a first flight took off from Rome, Italy carrying migrants to Sweden. This solidarity is based on the shared understanding by Member States that geography should not determine the burden to bear;
- The EU has launched a crisis management operation (EUNAVFOR MED)— which aims at disrupting the business model of migrant smuggling in the Southern Central Mediterranean and has now entered the second, active phase. In this context let me thank for a constructive approach of the US in the UN Security Council on that issue;
- The EU has led the international humanitarian response since the beginning of the Syria crisis with more than €4.1 billion mobilised. Member States and the Commission announced on September 23rd an additional contribution of €1 billion to UN agencies and the World Food Program;
- The EU has established the EU regional Trust Fund for Syria (Madad Fund) with more than €500 million funding in order to enhance resilience in refugee hosting countries around Syria and provide opportunities for refugees to pursue livelihoods, have access to education and labour market;
- The EU is also setting up the Emergency Trust Fund For Africa focused on addressing the root causes of irregular migration from Africa;
- The EU is also significantly strengthening its support to transit countries in the Western Balkan which are under enormous pressure in handling the refugee flows. An important high-level conference on the Eastern Mediterranean/Western Balkan migratory route took place recently in Luxembourg (8 October);
- We step up our support to and strategic dialogue with Turkey, which is a key country in the region hosting a large bulk of the refugees. We have just negotiated with Turkish authorities a Joint Action Plan aimed at addressing the phenomenon in a spirit of partnership and burden-sharing. The EU will make available €1 billion for refugee-related actions in 2015–16, in order to support refugees and their Turkish host communities and strengthen cooperation to prevent irregular migration;
- The High Representative is holding High Level Dialogues on migration with key Third countries in order to identify leverage and enhance cooperation in the area of migration. Cooperation on return and readmission of those who are not entitled to stay is also an important aspect in this context;
- An effective response to the current requires us to work closely together, as the international community, to address both its consequences but also the root causes. Since the beginning of the crisis, we have worked closely with our international partners, including the US, to formulate a global response. We welcome considerable humanitarian assistance provided by the US authorities in the context of the refugee crisis so far. We hope that there will be opportunity to cooperate more with the US also in order to provide more resilience and opportunities for the refugees in the region. Appreciating the involvement of the US in the crisis, especially as regards resettlement, the UE is counting strongly on the US to heighten its efforts, including by expanding the resettlement quotas.

Next steps

Undoubtedly, the refugee crisis has generated major challenges for the European Union. We have been able to take major steps to build a common approach and common policies based on solidarity and responsibility. In order to deal with issues that have long been seen as internal affairs at the heart of their sovereignty, EU Member States have agreed to develop a strong and multi-dimensional EU response.

On November 11–12, European heads of state and government will convene with key African countries to tackle the roots of economic migration in Africa during the Valletta Summit on Migration.

On November 13, the EU-US Justice and Home Affairs Ministerial meeting will take place to discuss the matter in details and exchange experience and best practice in managing migratory flows.

Over the next 6 months, the European Commission will also bring forward new major legislative proposals to implement a robust system that will bear the test of time.

By December 2015, the Commission will come forward with a proposal to strengthen Frontex and enhance its mandate in the context of discussions over the development of a European Border and Coast Guard System, giving it the competence and financial resources it needs to run return operations and to support member States.

To reinforce the overall migration and asylum policy of the EU, the Commission will also table a proposal for a permanent resettlement scheme and further reform of the Dublin Regulation in March 2016.

In addition, the Commission will table a legal migration package including the revision of the Blue Card, the EU work permit for highly qualified workers, in March 2016.

The EU will also continue to provide protection to those who come to European as well as continue its efforts to establish safe and legal means for asylum seekers to seek protection in Europe without risking their lives, for instance through expanded resettlement. It is crucial to protect people in need of protection in a humane way—regardless of which EU Member State they arrive in. The EU and its Member States are firmly committed to the promotion and protection of the human rights of migrants. Despite the influx, we do not remove or return genuine refugees, we respect the fundamental rights of all persons arriving in the EU, and we invest major resources in saving lives at sea. No flow of refugees justifies the catastrophic humanitarian conditions that we have seen earlier this month. This is why we need better harmonised procedures, better cooperation and shared standards across the globe. This is why the involvement of Europe has been increasing.

We will also closely monitor how the situation evolves in Turkey and in other countries neighbouring Syria and further adapt our policies accordingly, keeping as a priority international protection and humanitarian assistance to those in need.

Despite the challenges which remain ahead of us, I strongly believe that the refugee crisis can actually make the European Union stronger and more resilient.

Thank you for this opportunity to discuss such an important issue with you.

Prior to arriving in the United States, David O'Sullivan served as the Chief Operating Officer of the European External Action Service. The EEAS supports the High Representative/Vice President of the European Commission, in fulfilling her mandate to ensure the consistency of the Union's external action. The EEAS also assists the President of the European Council and the President of the European Commission in the area of external relations.

David O'Sullivan was Director General for Trade from 2005 to 2010. Previously he was Secretary General of the European Commission from June 2000 to November 2005, Head of Cabinet of Commission President Romano Prodi and Director General for Education and Training. He started his career in the Irish Foreign Ministry and spent four years in the Commission Delegation in Tokyo. He also has extensive experience in EU social and employment policy.

David O'Sullivan has a background in economics, graduating from Trinity College, Dublin and having completed post graduate studies at the College of Europe, Bruges. He holds an Honorary Doctorate from the Dublin Institute of Technology. He is also a Member of the Consultative Board of the Institute for International Integration Studies at Trinity College, Dublin. He is a visiting Professor at the European College of Parma and was awarded Alumnus of the Year 2013 by the College of Europe, Bruges.

In June 2014, David O'Sullivan was awarded the EU Transatlantic Business Award by the American Chamber of Commerce. He was awarded an Honorary Doctorate from his Alma mater Trinity College, Dublin in December, 2014.

He is married with two children.

MATERIAL FOR
THE RECORD

72

RÉSUMÉ OF ANNE C. RICHARD

Anne C. Richard was sworn in as Assistant Secretary of State for Population, Refugees, and Migration on April 2, 2012. Prior to her appointment, Ms. Richard was the vice president of government relations and advocacy for the International Rescue Committee (IRC), an international aid agency that helps refugees, internally displaced and other victims of conflict. She was also a non-resident Fellow of the Center for Transatlantic Relations at Johns Hopkins University/SAIS and a board member of the Henry L. Stimson Center.

From 1999 to 2001, Ms. Richard was Director of the Secretary's Office of Resources, Plans and Policy at the State Department. From 1997 to 1999, she was the deputy chief financial officer of the Peace Corps. Earlier, she served as a Senior Advisor in the Deputy Secretary's Office of Policy and Resources at the State Department and as a Budget Examiner at the U.S. Office of Management and Budget.

From 1993 to 1994, Ms. Richard was an International Affairs Fellow of the Council on Foreign Relations and was part of the team that created the International Crisis Group. From 1985 to 1986, she was a fellow of the Robert Bosch Foundation in Germany. She first joined the U.S. government in 1984 as a Presidential Management Intern.

Ms. Richard has authored several monographs and reports and numerous opinion pieces on topics including: international coordination of foreign assistance; combating terrorism; strategies to make foreign aid more cost effective; and specific humanitarian crises from Haiti to South Sudan to Afghanistan.

Ms. Richard has a B.S. in Foreign Service from Georgetown University and an M.A. in Public Policy Studies from the University of Chicago. She has lived overseas in Austria, Germany and France. She is married with two children.

EXCERPT FROM CONGRESSIONAL RESEARCH SERVICE MEMORANDUM, DATED OCTOBER 15, 2015

SECURITY SCREENING

USCIS coordinates the security screening process for refugees. According to the agency, "the screening conducted on refugees is the most robust of any population processed by USCIS."[1] Comprehensive, step-by-step information on the security screening process is not publicly available. USCIS has provided CRS with the following description of the process for refugees generally and Syrian refugees, in particular:

A standard suite of required biographic and biometric security checks has been developed for all refugee applicants. Through close coordination with the federal law enforcement and intelligence communities, these checks are continually reviewed to identify potential enhancements and to develop approaches for specific populations that may pose particular threats. The biographic checks include vetting refugee data against the State Department's Consular Lookout and Support System (CLASS). CLASS is a biographic name check database used to access critical information for visa adjudication and is run on all refugee applicants. CLASS contains information from TECS (formerly the Treasury Enforcement Communication System), the Terrorist Screening Database (TSDB), the Department of Health and Human Services (HHS), the Drug Enforcement Agency (DEA), Interpol, and the Federal Bureau of Investigation (FBI). In addition, refugee applicants meeting certain criteria are subject to Security Advisory Opinions (SAOs), including law enforcement and intelligence communities checks. SAO checks are run on applicants who meet these criteria and are between the ages of 16 to 50. Refugee applicants are subject to a third biographic check referred to as the Interagency Check (IAC); the IAC consists of screening biographic data against a broader range of intelligence community holdings. IACs are run on applicants who are age 14 and older. The biometric (fingerprint) checks (for applicants ages 14–79) include screening against the holdings of the Federal Bureau of Investigation (FBI) Next Generation Identification (NGI), the Department of Homeland Security (DHS) Automated Biometric Identification System (IDENT), and the Department of Defense Automated Biometric Identification System (ABIS).

In addition to this standard suite of security checks, USCIS Headquarters staff are reviewing all Syrian refugee cases prior to DHS interview to identify potential national security concerns. For those cases with potential national security concerns, USCIS conducts open source and classified research on the facts presented in the refugee claim and synthesizes an evaluation for use by the interviewing officer. This information provides case-specific context relating to country conditions and regional activity and is used by the interviewing officer to develop lines of inquiry related to the applicant's eligibility and credibility. USCIS has also instituted Syria-specific training for officers adjudicating cases with Syrian applicants, which includes a classified briefing on country conditions.

USCIS is continuing to engage with the law enforcement and intelligence communities, including exploring training opportunities and potential screening enhancements, to ensure that refugee vetting for Syrian refugee applicants is as robust as possible.[2]

---

[1] E-mail from USCIS to CRS, July 15, 2015.
[2] Ibid.

74

COMMUNICATION FROM THE COMMISSION TO THE EUROPEAN PARLIAMENT, THE
EUROPEAN COUNCIL AND THE COUNCIL

MANAGING THE REFUGEE CRISIS: STATE OF PLAY OF THE IMPLEMENTATION OF THE
PRIORITY ACTIONSUNDER THE EUROPEAN AGENDA ON MIGRATION

I. INTRODUCTION

In the first nine months of the year, over 710,000 people [1]—refugees, displaced persons and other migrants—have made their way to Europe, a trend which is set to continue. This is a test for the European Union. The European Agenda on Migration presented by the Commission in May 2015 [2] set out the need for a comprehensive approach to migration management. Since then, a number of important measures have been introduced—including the adoption of two emergency schemes to relocate 160,000 people in clear need of international protection from the Member States most affected to other EU Member States. The ongoing refugee crisis, however, requires further, immediate action.

For this reason, on 23 September, the European Commission detailed a set of **priority actions** to implement the European Agenda on Migration to be taken within the next six months. [3] This included both short term actions to stabilise the current situation as well as longer term measures to establish a robust system that will bear the test of time.

The list of priority actions set out the key measures immediately required in terms of: (i) **operational measures;** (ii) **budgetary support** and (iii) **implementation of EU law.**

The list was endorsed by the informal meeting of Heads of State and Government of 23 September 2015. [4]

Three weeks later, this Communication sets out the ongoing progress in implementing the priority actions (see Annex 1). The European Council this week provides an opportunity for Heads of State or Government to make a clear and unambiguous commitment to starting a new phase in the EU's response to the refugee crisis: one of swift and determined implementation.

II. OPERATIONAL MEASURES

Effectively managing the pressure of migratory flows on some parts of the shared external Schengen border requires both responsibility and solidarity on the part of all Member States. The rapid roll-out of the 'hotspot' approach is providing support to the most affected Member States to ensure the proper reception, identification and processing of arrivals. In parallel, the measures proposed by the Commission and adopted by the Council **to relocate 160,000 people in clear need of international protection.** This will allow for a significant, if partial, reduction of the pressure on the most affected Member States. It is of crucial importance that these parallel measures will now be fully implemented, with the fingerprinting of all migrants, the prompt selection and relocation of asylum applicants and adequate reception capacities, accompanied by steps to prevent secondary movements and the immediate return to the country of relocation of relocated persons found in another Member State. The other essential component is action to secure swift return, voluntary or forced, of people not in need of international protection and who do not therefore qualify for relocation. The priority actions set out by the Commission focused heavily on the operational working of these measures.

II.1 Implementing the 'Hotspot' Approach

Well-functioning and effective migration management at the external borders which are under most pressure is key to restoring confidence in the overall system, and in particular in the Schengen area of free movement without internal border controls. Central to the EU's strategy and credibility is to demonstrate that the migration system can be restored to proper functioning, in particular by using **Migration Management Support Teams deployed in 'hotspots'** [5] to help Member States under the most intense pressure to fulfil their obligations and responsibilities. For the Support Teams to work they need a strong core of EU Agencies, the

---

[1] Frontex figures published on 13 October 2015.
[2] COM(2015) 240 final.
[3] COM(2015) 490 final.
[4] Statement available at http://www.consilium.europa.eu/en/press/press-releases/2015/09/23-statement-informal-meeting.
[5] A 'hotspot' is a section of the EU external border or a region with extraordinary migratory pressure which calls for reinforced and concerted support by EU Agencies.

closest of cooperation with the authorities in Italy and Greece, and the support of other Member States.

The Commission has sent special envoys to both Italy and Greece to provide practical coordination and support. In Greece, a dedicated team is working under the leadership of the Commission's Director-General of the Structural Reform Support Service, reporting directly to the President. This team has agreed a step-by-step approach to identify the 'hotspots', deploy the Support Teams, start relocations, resume returns, and reinforce the border. The same model of direct, real-time support and coordination is in place in Italy. This intensive, full-time support from the Commission has made a real difference in helping the two Member States to move to the implementation phase of relocation (see Annex 2 and Annex 3).

Both in Greece and in Italy, the Migration Management Support Teams are being set up and coordinated by European Regional Task Forces, following the increased deployment of the Agencies set out in the European Agenda on Migration. Frontex, the European Asylum Support Office (EASO), Europol, and Eurojust all participate. [6] As a result, they can respond immediately to the needs identified in roadmaps presented by Italy and Greece.

However, their work relies heavily on the support of Member States. **Frontex and EASO have both launched calls for contributions** to request human resources and technical equipment from Member States. In both cases, these calls constitute unprecedented numbers when compared to requests made by the Agencies in the past, reflecting the exceptional nature of the challenges currently faced by the most affected Member States: it is essential that other Member States respond positively, concretely and quickly to these calls.

Frontex's latest call requested 775 additional border guards, screeners, debriefers, and interpreters—all indispensable tasks for the effective management of the external borders of the European Union. The call was split into 670 officers—mainly for direct support to the 'hotspot' approach in Italy and Greece, covering estimated needs to the end of January 2016—and 105 guest officers to be deployed at various external land borders of the European Union.

EASO's latest call for over 370 experts is intended to cover the needs in Italy and Greece until the third quarter of 2017. These experts would support the asylum management authorities of the two Member States in the registration process, information tasks related to relocation and the detection of possible fraudulent documents.

The need for personnel and equipment was explicitly recognised at the informal meeting of EU Heads of State or Government in September—with a deadline of November to meet these needs.

However, so far, the commitments made by Member States fall far short of the real needs. As of 8 October, only six Member States [7] have responded to the call for contributions for EASO with 81 experts, out of the 374 needed. So far six Member States [8] have responded to the call from Frontex with 48 border officials. **Member States should rapidly submit their contributions to meet the Agencies' needs assessment.**

Italy has identified as 'hotspot' areas Augusta, Lampedusa, Porte Empedocle, Pozzallo, Taranto and Trapani (see Annex 5). The first Migration Management Support Team is up and running, in Lampedusa. This builds on a European Regional Task Force set up in June 2015, in Catania, Sicily. [9] The Support Team currently consists of two debriefing teams from Frontex, plus EASO experts both at the 'hotspot' and at a nearby centre used for relocation. Frontex has already deployed 42 guest officers, while EASO has deployed 6 experts.

For the 'hotspot' approach to be effective, an increase in reception capacities is essential, in order to host asylum seekers before they are relocated. There also needs to be adequate capacity to detain irregular migrants before a return decision is executed. Italy has expanded its reception capacities and now has first reception centres in the four identified 'hotspot' areas, capable of housing approximately 1,500 people. Capacity will be expanded to provide for an additional 1,000 places by the end of the year, bringing the overall first reception capacity up to 2,500.

---

[6] The representatives of these Agencies work together in shared offices, based in ports or specific reception centres, to coordinate the EU assistance to the national authorities in identification, registration and return as well as information and intelligence gathering, sharing and analysis to support criminal investigations of people-smuggling networks.

[7] Austria, Belgium, the Netherlands, Romania, Slovakia and Spain.

[8] Belgium, the Czech Republic, Lithuania, Portugal, Romania and Sweden.

[9] The Task Force involves Frontex, EASO, Europol, the EU naval operation EUNAVFORMED-SOPHIA and the Italian authorities.

Greece has identified five 'hotspot' areas, in Lesvos, Chios, Leros, Samos and Kos (see Annex 4). The European Regional Task Force is fully operational, based in Piraeus. The first Migration Management Support Team will be based around the 'hotspot' in Lesvos. Frontex has already deployed 53 experts: at present one EASO staff member is permanently stationed in Greece to help organise the deployment of EASO experts.

Greece has expanded its reception capacities and now has seven first reception centres, screening centres and temporary facilities in four of the identified hotspot areas (Lesvos, Chios, Samos and Leros), capable of housing approximately 2,000 people. Capacity is being expanded further. [10]

Part of the reception needs in 'hotspot' areas is linked to the identification and registration of irregular migrants who are not in clear need of international protection, and thus do not qualify for relocation. This requires sufficient capacity to be available with the facilities to prevent irregular migrants absconding.

II.2 Rolling out the Relocation scheme

On 14 September, the Council adopted the Commission's proposal for a Decision [11] to relocate 40,000 people in clear need of international protection from Italy and Greece. This was followed a week later by the Decision, A[12] again based on a Commission proposal, to relocate 120,000 people in clear need of international protection from Italy, Greece and other Member States directly affected by the refugee crisis. The Migration Management Support Teams are the tools to ensure that this relocation can happen at the Union's external borders.

Both Decisions require immediate follow up from the EU institutions, the Member States under pressure and the Member States who are committed to hosting relocated people.

On 1 October, the European Commission brought together over 80 delegates from the Member States, the EU Agencies, the International Organisation for Migration and the United Nations High Commissioner for Refugees (UNHCR) in a **Relocation and Resettlement Forum** to take forward practical implementation. Italy and Greece presented their roadmaps for relocation at the Forum—outlining measures in the area of asylum, first reception and return, as well as the steps they would take in the weeks to come to ensure a full roll-out of the relocation scheme.

The first relocations of people in clear need of protection have taken place, but much work is still needed to ensure that a substantial flow of several hundreds of relocations per month quickly follows. All Member States were asked to identify national contact points at home: so far, 21 Member States have identified national contact points. [13] They have also been asked to send liaison officers, if relevant, to Italy and Greece. So far, 22 Member States have dispatched such officers. [14]

An essential part of the relocation chain is that adequate reception capacity exists in the receiving Member States to accommodate the relocated persons. So far, only six Member States have notified this reception capacity they have made available to host relocated people. [15] **All Member States should complete this notification by the end of October.**

---

[10] For example, a temporary facility for 300-400 places in Kos by the end of the year.

[11] Council Decision (EU) 2015/1523 of 14 September 2015 establishing provisional measures in the area of international protection for the benefit of Italy and of Greece (OJ L 239, 15.9.2015, p. 146).

[12] Council Decision (EU) 2015/1601 of 22 September 2015 establishing provisional measures in the area of international protection for the benefit of Italy and of Greece (OJ L 248, 24.9.2015, p. 80).

[13] Austria, Belgium, Bulgaria, Croatia, Cyprus, Finland, France, Germany, Greece, Hungary, Italy, Latvia, Luxembourg, Malta, Poland, Portugal, Romania, Slovakia, Slovenia, Spain, Sweden.

[14] From Austria, Belgium, Croatia, Cyprus, Czech Republic, Estonia, Finland, France, Germany, Ireland, Latvia, Lithuania, Luxembourg, Malta, the Netherlands, Poland, Portugal, Romania, Spain, Slovakia, Sweden for Italy and Slovenia for both Italy and Greece.

[15] Austria, France, Germany, Luxembourg, Sweden and Spain.

FIRST EFFECTIVE RELOCATION OF PEOPLE IN CLEAR NEED OF INTERNATIONAL
PROTECTION

On 9 October 2015, a first flight left from Rome taking 19 Eritreans to start a new life in Sweden. Five women and 14 men left from Ciampino airport in the presence of Migration and Home Affairs Commissioner Dimitris Avramopoulos, Luxembourg Foreign Affairs Minister Jean Asselborn and Italian Minister of the Interior Angelino Alfano. It was an important symbolic moment which marked the start of a new, European approach to the way we treat asylum applications. However, beyond symbolism, relocations now need to become systematic, routine business in Italy and in Greece.

The first flight was the result of intensive preparatory work on the ground by the Italian and Swedish authorities, by Frontex and other EU agencies, by local NGOs, and by the special envoys which the European Commission has deployed. Tireless efforts have ensured that the system is operational, and the necessary registration and processing can be done at each step of the way.

Outreach to the Eritrean community was crucial in ensuring the success of the first exercise. Initially asylum seekers were reluctant to be registered because they did not trust the system. It has taken a lot of effort over the past weeks from the Commission envoys on the ground, working with the UNHCR and local NGOs, to convince the first set of people that they really would be relocated.

Trust in the system is increasing, however, particularly since the first exercise was carried out. There are now queues of people wanting to register in Lampedusa and Villa Sikania. There are over 100 Eritreans already identified as candidates for relocation.

It is now crucial that further relocation exercises follow suit, particularly to avoid a 'bottleneck' of relocation candidates accumulating.

The successful transfer of the first groups of persons under the relocation exercises is an important first step. These exercises now need to be put on a firm and ongoing footing, at a sufficient scale. **All Member States should now provide the Commission with their clear commitments as to the number of people they will relocate from now until the end of the year**, bearing in mind the urgency of the challenge.

II.3 Resettlement

Resettlement of people in need of international protection directly from third countries both responds to the EU's humanitarian obligations, and provides a safe alternative for refugees as compared to taking the perilous journey to Europe themselves. At the Relocation and Resettlement Forum on 1 October, Member States confirmed the commitments made in July to welcome over 20,000 refugees in the next two years in this way. A Resettlement Workshop on 2 October developed practical solutions to ensure the effective application of resettlement. The first resettlements have now taken place. [16] **Member States should now provide the Commission with information on the number of people they will resettle over the next six months, and from where.**

II.4 Return and Readmission

A key element in the interlocking mechanisms which make up the EU asylum system is ensuring that those who do not have a right to international protection are effectively **returned**. At present, far too few return decisions are being implemented in practice and smuggling networks exploit this to attract migrants who are not in need of international protection. The more effective the return system becomes, the less chance that smugglers can persuade people that they will be able to 'slip through the net' if identified as not in need of international protection.

At the October 2015 Justice and Home Affairs Council, Member States endorsed the EU action plan on return proposed by the Commission. [17] The focus is now on swift and effective follow-up.

---

[16] 132 Syrians staying in neighbouring countries have already been resettled under the scheme agreed on 20 July 2015 to the Czech Republic (16), Italy (96), and Liechtenstein (20).
[17] COM(2015) 453 final.

Italy has recently carried out two return operations—28 Tunisians were returned from Italy to Tunisia and 35 Egyptians were returned to Egypt. One joint return operation, coordinated by Frontex, is foreseen in October from Italy and two from Greece. The frequency of these operations needs to be increased.

Ensuring effective returns is a core part of the work of the Migration Management Support Teams in 'hotspot' locations.

This also requires efficient systems to be in place inside the EU for issuing and enforcing return decisions. Concrete steps have been taken over the past month to develop a system of integrated return management and to make use of the EU's information exchange systems to include return decisions and entry bans. Member States' return agencies must also be given the necessary resources to perform their role.

Returns can only be implemented if there is an agreement by the countries of origin to readmit the persons concerned. **Readmission** is an indispensable component of an effective migration policy. Those who return must be readmitted to their countries of origin. This requires a close partnership with third countries, using all available tools at our disposal. Member States and the Commission should work together to find the fine balance of pressure and incentives in their relation with third countries to increase the number of returns. To assist in the process, **it has been agreed that Member States deploy European Migration Liaison Officers in eleven countries by the end of 2015, but this deployment has not yet taken place.** [18] The High Representative/Vice-President has launched the first high-level dialogues with main countries of origin of irregular migration, and this will be followed up in a variety of broader dialogues with Ethiopia, Somalia, the African Union and the Sahel countries. **The immediate priority is to ensure that existing readmission agreements are effectively applied in practice.**

MAKING READMISSION WORK: PRACTICAL COOPERATION WITH PAKISTAN

The EU has a readmission agreement in place with Pakistan since 2012. Given the large numbers involved (see Annex 9)—for many years, Pakistan has been the fourth largest source of non-EU nationals found to be in the EU in an irregular way—this agreement is of particular importance. But the estimate is that only around 54% of Pakistani citizens receiving return decisions in the EU are returned. The effectiveness of the implementation of the Agreement varies significantly amongst Member States. A particular blockage was identified in Greece, resulting from disputes concerning documentation. Dedicated readmission discussions between the Commission, Greece and the Pakistani authorities this month aim to restart the returns process:

- Discussions on the application of the EU-Pakistan readmission agreement took place in Athens between Commission, Greek and
- Contacts between the EU Delegation in Islamabad and the Pakistani Ministry of Foreign Affairs took place on the same day;
- Commissioner Avramopoulos will travel to Islamabad on 29 October to discuss a joint plan on migration.

The result should be:
- A joint understanding on the application of the EU readmission agreement between Greece and Pakistan;
- Frontex will carry out a joint return operation for Pakistanis from Greece in November;
- The Commission will present an operational action plan for better migration management with Pakistan.

II.5 Other Ways to Support Member States

There are several other opportunities for Member States to call on the support of the EU to provide assistance in border and migration management but which still have not been fully exploited.

---

[18] Council conclusions 8 October 2015: "Cooperation with the countries of origin and transit is key to successful return operations. In the short term, the EU will explore the synergies of the EU diplomacy on the ground, through the EU delegations, and in particular through the European Migration Liaison Officers (EMLOs), to be deployed by the end of 2015 to Egypt, Morocco, Lebanon, Niger, Nigeria, Senegal, Pakistan, Serbia, Ethiopia, Tunisia, Sudan, Turkey and Jordan."

Member States can request the deployment of **Rapid border intervention teams** (RABIT) to provide immediate border guard support in cases of urgent or exceptional migratory pressure. The Commission considers that the circumstances faced by Greece over the last few months have been exactly the circumstances for which the Teams were devised. Neither Greece nor Italy has so far triggered the mechanism.

The **EU Civil Protection Mechanism** [19] can be activated by a country if it considers itself to be overwhelmed by a crisis. The Mechanism relies on voluntary contributions from Member States (including expertise, equipment, shelter, and medical supplies). Member States were asked last month to notify the Commission of the assets which can be held ready to deploy to help refugees. Only eight Member States [20] have notified that they have—limited—civil protection assets or experts they would be prepared to deploy still this year, should a request be made. **The Commission reiterates the need for Member States to support the mechanism with substantial contributions.**

The Mechanism has been activated twice in 2015 to assist Hungary,[21] and once to assist Serbia,[22] in responding to the urgent needs caused by an unprecedented inflow of refugees and migrants.

It should also be recalled that the support of Member States through the **Frontex Joint Operations TRITON and POSEIDON** continues to provide day-by-day support to the management of the external borders, rescuing thousands of migrants and refugees in the process. Currently 17 Member States are providing assets to TRITON, 18 Member States to POSEIDON. [23] However, the assets made available still fall short of what is needed.

Progress Made

- First 'hotspot' working in Lampedusa (Italy).
- First 'hotspot' in Lesvos (Greece) to be operational in the coming days.
- Relocations to other Member States have started.
- Migration Management Support Teams are operational.
- The first resettlements have taken place.
- Frontex supporting return missions.

Next Steps

- Six 'hotspots' in total to be operational in Italy by the end of the year.
- Five 'hotspots' in total to be operational in Greece by the end of the year.
- Member States to meet calls for experts and equipment to support the Migration Management Support Teams to allow the Support Teams to be rolled out in full.
- Member States to notify how many relocation and resettlement places they will provide, and specify their reception capacity.
- Returns to Pakistan from Greece to restart.
- Member States to provide adequate resources for Frontex Joint Operations TRITON and POSEIDON.

III. BUDGETARY SUPPORT

Three weeks ago, the Commission committed to reinforcing financial support immediately. Since then, the Commission has proposed amending budgets to increase financial resources devoted to tackling the refugee crisis by an additional **€ 1.7 billion for 2015 and 2016.**

This includes:

- Additional emergency assistance already in 2015 under the Asylum, Migration and Immigration Fund and the Internal Security Fund-Borders (€100 million) (see Annex 8);
- Reinforcement of the three key Agencies by 120 posts (60 posts for FRONTEX, 30 for EASO and 30 for EUROPOL);

---

[19] The Mechanism can mobilise various types of in-kind assistance, including expertise, equipment, shelter, and medical supplies.

[20] Belgium, Cyprus, Finland, Sweden, Slovakia, the Czech Republic, Lithuania, Latvia.

[21] These requests are now closed.

[22] This request is still open.

[23] Malta, Portugal, the Netherlands, France, Norway, Spain, Greece, Poland, Romania, the United Kingdom, Germany, Denmark, the Czech Republic, Bulgaria and Latvia in the case of TRITON, Denmark, the Czech Republic, Norway, Sweden, Portugal, Poland, Latvia, Germany, Croatia, the Netherlands, Finland, Italy, France, Spain, Belgium, the United Kingdom and Romania in the case of POSEIDON.

- Additional funding for the European Neighbourhood Instrument (€300 million) and redeployment of other EU funds so that the EU Trust Fund for Syria can reach at least €500 million this year;
- An increase of the funding for Humanitarian Aid of €500 million (€200 million in 2015 and €300 million in 2016) to help refugees directly, notably through UNHCR, the World Food Programme and other relevant organisations to help refugees' essential needs, like food and shelter;
- €600 million in additional commitments for 2016 to increase emergency funding on migration issues (€94 million), to support the relocation package (€110 million), increased human and financial resources for FRONTEX, EASO and EUROPOL (about €86 million to assist on returns and in the 'hotspot' areas, as well as reinforcement of the Agencies), and additional funding to help Member States most affected by the refugee crisis (€310 million).

In total this means that the available funding to address the refugee crisis will amount to **€9.2 billion in 2015 and 2016**.

The European Parliament and the Council have acted swiftly to adopt the changes to the 2015 budget. The Commission has now adopted amendments for the 2016 budget and **calls upon the budgetary authority to make a similar commitment to fast-track the 2016 budget.**

It is crucial that national spending is now deployed to reinforce the overall European effort in addition to this substantial reinforcement of migration-related spending under the EU budget. This was recognised by the EU Heads of State and Government on 23 September, which highlighted the need for **national governments to contribute and match the EU funding** in the efforts made to:

- Support the urgent needs of refugees through **UNHCR, the World Food Programme** [24] and other agencies, to reach at least €1 billion. With the EU budget providing €200 million in additional support this year and €300m next year, this requires a commitment of €500 million from national budgets.

Since 23 September, ten Member States [25] have committed to additional contribution, with the total reaching around €275 million. But in reality, over 80% of this has been pledged by only two Member States, the United Kingdom and Germany. **This still leaves a shortfall of over €225 million.**

- Support a substantial increase in the **EU's Regional Trust Fund responding to the Syria crisis**. The Commission calls on Member States to match the €500 million from the EU budget.

However, despite the fact that Syria is at the core of today's crisis and that this Trust Fund offers a flexible and swift delivery tool, the response so far from Member States has been minimal, with just two Member States, Italy pledging €3 million and Germany pledging €5 million. **This leaves an almost total shortfall of €492 million.**

- Support with national contributions the **Emergency Trust Fund for stability and addressing the root causes of irregular migration and displaced persons in Africa.** The Commission considers that national contributions should match the €1.8 billion EU funding. Again, support committed so far has been negligible, with only three Member States at present, Luxembourg, Germany and Spain, pledging €3 million each. Six Member States [26] have informally confirmed their contributions but without clear figures. Four others [27] have said that it is "very likely" that they will contribute and four [28] are still considering it. Two non-EU countries [29] have informally suggested they might pledge in total around €9 million. **This leaves a huge shortfall of €1.791 million.**

Financial resources are an indispensable part of how we can both address the immediate plight of refugees and start to tackle the root causes. It is imperative that the shortfall between the needs identified by the European Council and the reality of what just a few Member States have so far pledged is swiftly redressed (see Annex 7).

---

[24] Four Member States—the United Kingdom, Germany, the Netherlands and Sweden—rank in the top 10 donors to the World Food Programme in 2015 (source: World Food Programme, 6 October 2015).

[25] Cyprus, Czech Republic, Finland, Germany, Italy, Latvia, Luxembourg, Poland, Spain and the United Kingdom

[26] Belgium, Denmark, France, Italy, Malta and the United Kingdom.

[27] Austria, the Netherlands, Finland and Sweden.

[28] The Czech Republic, Estonia, Latvia and Greece.

[29] Norway and Switzerland.

Progress Made

- Adoption by the European Parliament and the Council of the reinforcement of €800 million to support refugees and migration policies in 2015, as proposed by the Commission.
- Further reinforcement of €900 million for 2016 now before the budgetary authority.

Next Steps

- European Parliament and Council should adopt the changes to the 2016 budget, as proposed by the Commission.
- Member States need to complete the pledge of €500 million in support for humanitarian aid to refugees to reach €1 billion.
- Member States to match the €500 million funding from the EU budget to the EU Syria Trust Fund and the €1.8 billion in EU funding for the EU Trust Fund for Africa.

In this context, questions have arisen about the treatment under the **Stability and Growth Pact** of expenditure incurred to manage the refugee crisis. The Commission has confirmed that, if it received a specific request from a Member State, it would examine whether and how this could be accommodated under the existing rules of the Stability and Growth Pact. This includes the flexibility that has been imbedded in the Pact to react to unforeseen circumstances and unusual events.

This assessment would need to be made on a case-by-case basis as part of the analysis of national fiscal documents. It would need to be based on evidence of the net costs incurred, in line with the agreed methodology for applying the Pact.

IV. IMPLEMENTATION OF EU LAW

The Common European Asylum System is based on helping people in need of international protection and returning migrants who have no right to stay on EU territory. To make this a reality, the EU now has a strong set of common rules on asylum and irregular migration. But these rules have to be properly applied.

One example of the Commission's efforts to promote effective implementation is in the area of return, where the Commission has been helping Member States to understand the consequences of the rules. The Commission has held dedicated dialogues with Member States to highlight steps that need to be taken to meet the obligation to enforce return. Member States should ensure the physical availability of an irregular migrant for return and use detention, as a legitimate measure of last resort, where it is necessary to avoid that irregular migrants abscond. As long as there is a reasonable likelihood of removal, prospects for such removal should not be undermined by a premature ending of detention. Finally, both the swiftness of decision-making, and the availability of staff and sufficient detention capacity, can have a key impact on the practical implementation of return decisions.

Since August, the Commission has sent **administrative letters** to five Member States concerning the Eurodac Regulation on fingerprinting, and ten concerning the correct implementation of the Return Directive. All Member States concerned replied on the Eurodac Regulation , and the Commission is now assessing the replies to see if they are sufficient or if infringement proceedings should be launched. On the Return Directive, only one response[30] has been received so far: the Commission awaits the remaining responses and will swiftly assess the situation. A further administrative letter has been addressed to one Member State concerning the compliance with the Asylum Procedures Directive, the Reception Conditions Directive and the Schengen Borders Code.

In respect of the decision **on 40 potential or actual infringement decisions adopted in September**, concerning the Asylum Procedures Directive, the Reception Conditions Directive and the Qualifications Directive, in addition to the 34 cases opened before then, the Commission has not received any responses so far. Given the particular importance of this legislation, Member States are urged to respond as early as possible within the two month period.

The Commission will continue to pursue infringement procedures swiftly and effectively, where necessary, to ensure full compliance with EU legislation in this area (see Annex 6).

The priority actions identified in September stressed the need to devote particular attention to **Greece**. Member States have not been able to return asylum seekers to Greece since 2010–11. In 2010, the European Court of Human Rights ruled that there had been a number of violations of the European Convention on Human

---

[30] Italy

Rights. The European Court of Justice then confirmed that there could be no presumption that Member States respect the fundamental rights of asylum seekers if they return people to Greece under the Dublin system.

As noted above, the Commission has dedicated substantial resources to assisting Greece. Member States are now starting to add to these efforts. Significant progress has been made in a short space of time. With the Migration Management Support Teams up and running, the key deficiencies behind the effective suspension of Dublin transfers are being addressed—with reception facilities being expanded and a return being made to a robust system of asylum processing.

Progress so far has been encouraging and must continue. On this basis, **the Commission will assess the situation by 30 November 2015 and if all conditions are met, it will recommend to the European Council in December 2015 or in March 2016 to confirm the reinstatement of Dublin transfers to Greece.**

Several Member States have recently invoked the **temporary reintroduction of border controls** under the Schengen Border Code. This can be justified in exceptional crisis situations and notably for serious threats to public policy or internal security in a given Member State. But it can never be more than a short-term measure before the situation is stabilised.

The Commission is currently finalising its assessment of the situation by adopting an opinion on the prolongation of temporary border controls by Germany, Austria and Slovenia on the basis of the Schengen Border Code.

Progress made

- The Commission is addressing deficiencies by Member States in the full transposition and implementation of EU law.
- Reception facilities are being expanded and conditions for a correct asylum system and processing are being put in place in Greece.

Next steps

- The Commission will ensure active and swift follow-up of all infringement proceedings in asylum and return.
- The Commission will assess by 30 November 2015 the situation concerning Dublin transfers to Greece.

V. THE EXTERNAL DIMENSION

The European Agenda on Migration underlined that a successful migration policy must inescapably work outside as well as inside the Union. Europe must always welcome those in need of protection. But it is in everyone's interests that the crises which force refugees to leave their homes and travel in great danger are tackled at their roots.

At the core of the priority actions and the joint Communication of the Commission and the High Representative/Vice-President last month [31] was putting migration at the top of the EU's external concerns. This has been shown through the commitments to extra funding set out above. But the diplomatic offensive now under way has also put migration at the centre of bilateral, regional and multilateral dialogue.

Turkey is a pivotal partner. Together with Lebanon and Jordan, it has borne the brunt of the humanitarian effort to shelter Syrian refugees. Its geographical position makes it the dominant channel for migrants arriving in the Western Balkans. Turkey has shown that it is capable of taking decisive action to combat smuggling. The detailed Action Plan on Migration handed by President Juncker to President Erdogan on 5 October set out a series of concrete measures covering both support of refugees, migrants, and their hosting communities, as well as strengthening cooperation to prevent irregular migration. It sets out short, medium, and longer term actions. **The Commission is now in active discussions with the Turkish authorities in order to finalise the Action Plan.**

Cooperation with Turkey was also a key aspect of the **High-level Conference on the Eastern Mediterranean—Western Balkans Route** convened on 8 October by the High Representative/Vice-President and the Luxembourg Presidency. This meeting agreed a series of practical steps to foster a more effective cooperation with partner countries along the route, including by supporting countries of first asylum and of transit, as well as underlining the broader issues of tackling root causes and fighting smuggling. [32]

---

[31] JOIN(2015) 40 of 9 September 2015
[32] This document can be found by following the link : http://www.consilium.europa.eu/en/press/press-releases/2015/10/08-western-balkans-route-conference-declaration/

The High Representative/Vice-President has been engaged in extensive diplomatic contacts with a view to finding an agreement to the crisis in Libya. These efforts, political and financial, have been deployed in support of the Special Representative of the UN Secretary General, Bernardino Léon, who, on 8 October, presented a final text of the Libyan Political Agreement to all participants in the political dialogue. The focus is now on having this agreement endorsed by the parties, in which case, the EU stands ready with a substantial and immediate package of support to a new government of National Accord that will benefit the Libyan population. The Foreign Affairs Council of 12 October adopted conclusions in this respect.

On 7 October, the **EU military operation in the Southern Mediterranean—EUNAVFOR MED Operation Sophia**—moved to its second phase in international waters, after having successfully fulfilled the objectives of phase 1 (surveillance and assessment of smuggling and trafficking networks), and contributing to the rescue of more than 3,000 people. It will now be able to conduct boarding, search, seizure and diversion, on the high seas, of vessels suspected of being used for human smuggling or trafficking, and will contribute to bringing suspected smugglers to justice. This represents a key development in disrupting the business model of traffickers/smugglers and received an important political endorsement from UN Security Council Resolution 2240 adopted on 9 October.

Under the chairmanship of the High Representative/Vice-President, the Foreign Affairs Council adopted conclusions on the **Syria** crisis on 12 October, on the basis of which the EU will enhance the level of its engagement in support of UN-led international efforts to find a political solution to the conflict. The High Representative/Vice-President is actively engaged with all of the key regional and international actors, including Russia, US, Saudi Arabia, Iran, Turkey and Iraq. The EEAS has taken measures to strengthen support to the political opposition inside and outside Syria as a party to a transition process and to continue to facilitate the rapprochement and unification of its numerous political and military segments behind a common strategy. On 7 and 9 September, the EEAS together with the UN Special Envoy, Staffan de Mistura, conducted detailed consultations with mediation practitioners, notably from Russia, Iran, Egypt and Saudi Arabia and Syria envoys from the Member States. The EU is also active in some of the working groups established by the Small Group of the Global Coalition against Da'esh, namely on stabilization, foreign terrorist fighters, counter-financing. Implementation of the EU regional strategy for Syria and Iraq as well as the Da'esh threat is on-going.

Migration was a key theme discussed by representatives of the EU institutions and of the Member States in the 70th **United Nations General Assembly** at the end of September. In this context, the need for a more proactive response and enhanced engagement by the international community to deal with the challenges of migration and human mobility was stressed, notably with regard to the Syrian refugee crisis.

The EU Action Plan against **migrant smuggling** presented in May[33] is now being implemented—as well as law enforcement operations both within and outside the EU—for example, campaigns are under way in Ethiopia and Niger to prevent smuggling at the source.

A major focus in the new priority on migration issues in the next month will be the **Valletta Summit on Migration** (11–12 November). This Summit is the subject of intensive preparation with African partners. It will represent an opportunity to show that both the EU and its African partners can deliver tangible action to address the root causes of irregular migration and to ensure orderly, safe, regular and responsible migration and mobility of people. Fundamental to such partnerships is that the EU must support its partners—with financial assistance, with expertise, with the confidence to work together and demonstrate a common effort. As such, its success is inextricably linked to a joint effort to deliver a major financial commitment to the EU Emergency Trust Fund for Africa (see above under point III).

Progress Made

- A series of high-level meetings by the High Representative/Vice-President and Commissioners have given meaning to the new diplomatic offensive on migration.
- EUNAVFOR MED operation Sophia fulfilled objectives of phase 1.

Next Steps

- Finalising the Action Plan with Turkey.

---

[33] COM(2015) 285 final

84

- High level dialogues foreseen by the High Representative/Vice-President with Ethiopia, the African Union and Somalia on 20–21 October.
- EUNAVFOR MED operation Sophia implementing its phase 2.
- EU to support a new government of National Accord in Libya.
- EU to enhance level of engagement in support of UN-led international efforts to find a political solution to the conflict in Syria.
- Valletta Summit on Migration.

VI. CONCLUSION

The operational and budgetary steps set out above are designed to provide the support needed to bring the EU's migration system back into an orderly approach where the rules are properly applied and the system is robust enough to react to the inevitable peaks in migration. An indispensable part of restoring stability is the external border. This is at the heart of the **Commission's commitment to bring forward before the end of the year proposals to develop a fully operational European Border and Coast Guard**, as a recognition that Member States must be supported more strongly in the challenge of managing Europe's external borders.

SUMMARY OF SPECIFIC CONCLUSIONS

- Member States should rapidly submit their contributions to meet the EU Agencies' needs assessment for the implementation of the "Hotspot" approach;
- Italy and Greece should increase their reception capacities;
- Member States should notify their reception capacity to host relocated people;
- Member States should provide clear commitments as to the number of people they will relocate from now until the end of the year;
- Member States should now provide the Commission with information on the number of people they will resettle over the next six months and from where;
- Member States should swiftly implement the EU action plan on return proposed by the Commission, for an effective system of return at EU level;
- European Migration Liaison Officers should be deployed by the EU in eleven third countries by the end of 2015,
- Member States should support the EU Civil Protection Mechanism with substantial contributions;
- Member States should make available sufficient assets for Frontex joint operations TRITON and POSEIDON;
- Member States should contribute to and match the EU funding in the efforts made to support the UNHCR, World Food Programme and other international organisations, the EU Trust Fund for Syria and the EU Trust Fund for Africa;
- The European Parliament and the Council should adopt the draft amending budget for 2016, as proposed by the Commission;
- The Commission will continue to pursue swiftly and effectively infringement procedures, where necessary, to ensure full compliance with the acquis in the area of Asylum and Return;
- The Commission will assess by 30 November 2015 if all conditions are met to recommend to the European Council in December 2015 or in March 2016 to confirm the reinstatement of Dublin transfers to Greece;
- The Commission will finalise its opinion on the prolongation of temporary controls by Germany, Austria and Slovenia on the basis of the Schengen Border Code;
- The Commission will finalise the Action Plan with Turkey.

List of Annexes

Annex 1: Follow-up of the Priority Actions
Annex 2: Greece—State of Play Report from 11 October 2015
Annex 3: Italy—State of Play Report from 11 October 2015
Annex 4: Map of the 'Hotspots' designated in Greece
Annex 5: Map of the 'Hotspots' designated in Italy
Annex 6: Implementing the Common European Asylum System
Annex 7: Member States' financial pledges since 23 September 2015

85

Annex 8: Financial Support to Member States under the Asylum, Migration and Integration Fund and the Internal Security Fund
Annex 9: The functioning of the EU-Pakistan Readmission Agreement 2012–2014

FROM: GENERAL SECRETARIAT OF THE EUROPEAN COUNCIL   TO: DELEGATIONS

SUBJECT: EUROPEAN COUNCIL MEETING, 15 OCTOBER 2015—CONCLUSIONS

MIGRATION

1. Tackling the migration and refugee crisis is a common obligation which requires a comprehensive strategy and a determined effort over time in a spirit of solidarity and responsibility. The orientations agreed by Heads of State or Government on 23 September focused on the most pressing issues. Their implementation is advancing rapidly, as evidenced by work undertaken within the Council and by the Commission report of 14 October. This will be kept under close review, including as concerns the financial pledges and possible further needs.

2. Today, the European Council set out the following further orientations:

Cooperating with third countries to stem the flows

a) welcomes the joint Action Plan with Turkey as part of a comprehensive cooperation agenda based on shared responsibility, mutual commitments and delivery. Successful implementation will contribute to accelerating the fulfilment of the visa liberalisation roadmap towards all participating Member States and the full implementation of the readmission agreement. Progress will be assessed in spring 2016. The EU and its Member States stand ready to increase cooperation with Turkey and step up their political and financial engagement substantially within the established framework. The accession process needs to be re-energized with a view to achieving progress in the negotiations in accordance with the negotiating framework and the relevant Council conclusions.

The European Council expressed its condolences to the people of Turkey following the Ankara bomb attack and pledged its support to fight terrorism;

b) ensure effective and operational follow up to the High-level Conference on the Eastern Mediterranean/Western Balkans Route, with particular emphasis on the management of migratory flows and the fight against criminal networks;

c) achieve concrete operational measures at the forthcoming Valletta Summit with African Heads of State or Government, focusing, in a fair and balanced manner, on effective return and readmission, dismantling of criminal networks and prevention of illegal migration, accompanied by real efforts to tackle root causes and to support the African socio-economic development together with a commitment concerning continued possibilities for legal migration;

d) explore possibilities for developing safe and sustainable reception capacities in the affected regions and providing lasting prospects and adequate procedures for refugees and their families, including through access to education and jobs, until return to their country of origin is possible;

e) ask Member States to further contribute to the efforts made to support UNHCR, World Food Programme and other agencies, as well as to support the EU's Regional Trust Fund responding to the Syria crisis and the EU Trust Fund for Africa.

Strengthening the protection of the EU's external borders (building on the Schengen acquis)

f) work towards the gradual establishment of an integrated management system for external borders;

g) make full use of the existing Frontex mandate, including as regards the deployment of Rapid Border Intervention Teams;

h) in accordance with the distribution of competences under the Treaty, in full respect of the national competence of the Member States, enhance the mandate of Frontex in the context of discussions over the development of a European Border and Coast Guard System, including as regards the deployment of Rapid Border Intervention Teams in cases where Schengen evaluations or risk analysis demonstrate the need for robust and prompt action, in cooperation with the Member State concerned;

i) devise technical solutions to reinforce the control of the EU's external borders to meet both migration and security objectives, without hampering the fluidity of movement;

j) welcome the Commission's intention to rapidly present a package of measures with a view to improving the management of our external borders.

Responding to the influx of refugees in Europe and ensuring returns

k) in accordance with the decisions taken so far, press ahead with the establishment of further hotspots within the agreed timeframe to ensure the identification, registration, fingerprinting and reception of applicants for international protection and other migrants and at the same time ensure relocation and returns. Member States will support these efforts to the full, in the first place by meeting the calls for expertise from Frontex and EASO for the Migration Management Support Teams to work in hotspot areas and by the provision of necessary resources;

l) further to the first successful relocations, proceed rapidly with the full implementation of the decisions taken so far on relocation as well as our commitments on resettlement and on the functioning of hotspots;

m) at the same time step up implementation by the Member States of the Return Directive and, before the end of the year, create a dedicated return office within Frontex in order to scale up support to Member States;

n) enlarge the Frontex mandate on return to include the right to organise joint return operations on its own initiative, and enhance its role regarding the acquisition of travel documents for returnees;

o) promote the acceptance by third countries of an improved European return laissez-passer as the reference document for return purposes;

p) effectively implement all readmission commitments, whether undertaken through formal readmission agreements, the Cotonou Agreement or other arrangements;

q) further increase leverage in the fields of return and readmission, using where appropriate the "more-for-more" principle. In this regard, the Commission and the High Representative will propose, within six months, comprehensive and tailor-made incentives to be used vis-à-vis third countries.

3. The orientations set out above represent a further important step towards our comprehensive strategy, consistent with the right to seek asylum, fundamental rights and international obligations. There are however other important priority actions that require further discussions in the relevant fora, including the Commission proposals. And there is a need for continuing reflection on the overall migration and asylum policy of the EU. The European Council will keep developments under review.

Syria and Libya

4. The European Council discussed political and military developments in Syria, including their impact on migration. The Assad regime bears the greatest responsibility for the 250.000 deaths of the conflict and the millions of displaced people. The European Council agreed on the need to focus on the fight against DAESH and other UN-designated terrorist groups in the framework of a united and coordinated strategy and a political process on the basis of the Geneva Communiqué of 2012. The EU is fully engaged in finding a political solution to the conflict in close cooperation with the UN and the countries of the region and calls on all parties involved to work to that effect. There cannot be a lasting peace in Syria under the present leadership and until the legitimate grievances and aspirations of all components of Syrian society are addressed. The European Council expressed its concern about the Russian attacks on the Syrian opposition and civilians and the risk of further military escalation.

5. As regards Libya, the European Council welcomed the announcement made by the UN and called on all parties to swiftly endorse it. The EU reiterates its offer of substantial political and financial support to the Government of National Accord as soon as it takes office.

OTHER ITEMS

6. The European Council took stock of the discussions on the Presidents' report on completing Europe's Economic and Monetary Union. The European Council reiterates that the process of completing the Economic and Monetary Union must be taken forward in full respect of the single market and in an open and transparent manner. The European Council will revert to these issues at its December meeting.

7. The European Council was informed about the process ahead concerning the UK plans for an (in/out) referendum. The European Council will revert to the matter in December.

8. The European Council welcomes the international and independent report, conducted by the Dutch Safety Board, published on 13 October into the downing of flight MH17 and supports the ongoing efforts to hold to account those responsible for the downing of MH17, in accordance with UNSC Resolution 2166.

SUBMITTED FOR THE RECORD BY METODIJA A. KOLOSKI, CO-FOUNDER AND PRESI-
DENT, UNITED MACEDONIAN DIASPORA, AND GAVIN KOPEL, UMD INTERNATIONAL
POLICY AND DIPLOMACY FELLOW

Challenges facing Macedonia in regards to Refugee Crisis

Macedonia has made great strides in the face of one of the most challenging crises of the 21st century, but no country can manage this crisis unilaterally. Lack of infrastructure led to isolated clashes between border police and refugees desperate to move through Macedonia on their way into Europe. In July, Macedonia passed legislation to allow the migrants 72 hours to pass through the country, allowing them to enter and exit the country legally. Special transportation has been arranged to move the refugees, a large number of police have been hired to register refugees and increase security, and the government is working in tandem with local and international NGOs to provide assistance to the refugees. Macedonia has done all this without closing its borders as other states have and is once again a regional leader in keeping up with the democratic and humanitarian values it shares with its western allies. However, growing costs are putting increased strain on an already heavily burdened economy. A prompt, unified response from the international community, led by the United States and the European Union, is needed to address not only the problems that led to this crisis but also the problems that have stemmed from it.

Macedonia, a country with a population of approximately two million people, is currently contending with an unprecedented number of migrants moving through its territory. From January to June, 124,000 migrants passed through Greece, a 750% increase over the previous year. In the short time from June 1st the rate at which migrants are entering Europe increased even more rapidly. Since June, over 140,000 migrants have passed through Greece. In this fourmonth period, more refugees have entered Macedonia through Greece than in all of last year. This number is only a fraction of the total number that has entered Europe this year. Only a tiny fraction of the refugees who enter Macedonia seek asylum there; only 550 have done so since the crisis began. A majority of the migrants who enter Europe through Greece proceed further into Europe through Macedonia's southern border near Gevgelija, a town with less than 16,000 inhabitants and vastly insufficient infrastructure to deal with such a high number of migrants. Recently, the southern border has seen up to 10,000 migrants crossing into the country per day.

Although Macedonia is a transit country for the refugees on their way deeper into Europe, the cost associated with the crisis is continually growing. At a recent American Bar Association- Rule of Law Initiative panel discussion on refugee crisis, Macedonian Ambassador to the United States Dr. Vasko Naumovski stated that the increased police force needed to maintain the security of the southern border is costing Macedonia over $100,000 per day. Macedonia is helping to assure the security of the European Union as the refugees pass through by registering and fingerprinting the refugees, reducing the risk of Islamic extremists slipping into Europe with the flow of refugees. As the number of people entering the country each day increases, the cost of this task increases substantially. Serbia's Ambassador Djerdj Matkovic, on the same panel, stated that the cost of simply feeding and providing water to the refugees is close to €20,000 per day, and with almost equal numbers of refugees moving through Macedonia, the costs are similar. With winter approaching, refugees will need heated shelters and additional services to keep them safe from the elements, which will drive up the cost of the crisis in the region even higher. Without increased foreign aid to address the growing burden on already taxed economies, the Balkans will not be able to maintain the services that are being provided for the refugees as they enter the countries.

The amount of funds that Macedonia receives from the EU to deal with this incredibly complicated issue is inadequate. Macedonia receives less than a quarter of the funding from the EU that Serbia does for migrant management, even though each country experiences a similar number of migrants. This figure is not an indictment of Serbia, but of the disjointed response from the international community. In addition to the €8.2 million package that Serbia is receiving through 2020 to expand its capacity for migrants, reform its asylum system and improve border security, it was recently granted €630,000 to address issues related to the influx of migrants and improve infrastructure including waste disposal, water and sanitation. In comparison to Serbia, the only funding Macedonia received from the EU was a mere €90,656. In stark contrast is the funding that Greece receives to address issues related to migration crisis. Despite the fact that most refugees cross Greece to enter Macedonia, Greece receives over 5,000 times more funding than Macedonia. In the period from 2014 to 2020, Greece will receive €474,192,915 to address issues related to this crisis. Norway, a non-EU member state, has given nearly as much aid unilaterally to the Balkans, namely Serbia and Macedonia, as the entirety of the EU with its aid package of NOK 60 million, nearly $7.5 million.

Resolution of the current crisis is viable only if responsibility is shared. No single country can rely solely on its own resources to solve a problem as complex as this. Macedonia has been a long-time friend and loyal ally to the United States since its own independence, and now the United States should be a leader in supporting Macedonia and its neighbors affected by the crisis and lead a common response with Europe with increased aid and technical assistance. If the EU wants to retain its position as a powerful global player that is genuinely committed to the promotion of peace, democracy and human rights, it must provide a unified and resolute response to the current migrant crisis. This includes providing adequate support to Macedonia and other non-EU states, which is crucial in ensuring that governments meet their obligations under international law to treat all migrants with dignity. Lastly, the United States must use its diplomatic resources-at-hand to bring upon a solution to Macedonia's NATO membership, so that the country can officially become a member at the 2016 Warsaw Summit.

○